PASTA GUSTO
Fabulous Sauces & Flavored Pastas

NORMAN KOLPAS

CONTEMPORARY
BOOKS

CHICAGO

Library of Congress Cataloging-in-Publication Data

Kolpas, Norman.
    Pasta gusto : fabulous sauces & flavored pastas / Norman Kolpas.
      p.   cm.
    Includes index.
    ISBN 0-8092-3726-1 (paper)
    1. Sauces.   2. Cookery (Pasta)   I. Title.
TX819.A1K63   1994
641.8'22—dc20
                                                94-11364
                                                CIP

Other cookbooks by Norman Kolpas

Pasta Presto
Pasta Light
Pasta Menus

Featured on cover: Shrimp Scampi with Bell Peppers and Pine Nuts (see Index).

Cover design by Georgene Sainati
Cover photograph by Brian Leatart
Foodstyling by Kim Wong
Dinner and flatware courtesy of Rosenthal
Linens by Anichini Linea Casa

Published by Contemporary Books, Inc.
Two Prudential Plaza, Chicago, Illinois 60601-6790
Manufactured in the United States of America
International Standard Book Number: 0-8092-3726-1
10   9   8   7   6   5   4   3   2   1

Contents

Acknowledgments

As always, thanks are due in large part to my editor, Nancy Crossman, for her support, insight, intelligence, patience, and good humor. All her colleagues at Contemporary Books who played a part in this book also deserve thanks, particularly Dawn Barker, Kristen Carr, Dana Draxten, Louise El, Jan Geist, Gigi Grajdura, Gerilee Hundt, Cyndy Raucci, Georgene Sainati, Terry Stone, and Kathy Willhoite. Thanks, too, to Brian Leatart and Norman Stewart for their usual brilliant job on the cover.

These recipes have evolved over meals served to guinea pigs too numerous to mention. Two of my tasters, however, get the biggest share of credit, especially for putting up with this book's long gestation: my wife, Katie, and our son, Jacob. Jake's special enthusiasm for colored and flavored pasta continues to inspire me.

Introduction

The phone call, insignificant on the face of it, nonetheless came to me as a revelation. One of my wife's cousins had dialed long-distance to ask me one plaintive question: "Somebody gave me some chocolate pasta," she said. "What do I do with it?"

Everywhere a food lover looks today, it seems that the shelves and refrigerated cases of supermarkets, delicatessens, and ethnic food shops—not to mention the menus of restaurants—offer up a wide array of fresh and dried pastas in a rainbow of colors. Spinach pasta, a long-standing tradition of the Italian kitchen and almost familiar enough to be counted an old friend. Carrot pasta. Jet-black squid ink pasta. Tomato pasta. Blushing red beet pasta. Pasta flecked with fresh herbs. And on and on.

The variety beguiles any food lover. But one question still lingers: What do I do with them?

That question from my wife's cousin stayed with me. It seems plain old flour-and-water or flour-egg-and-water pasta is regarded by most cooks as a blank slate, upon which you create a personality with your choice of sauce or topping. But flavored pasta confuses the issue. It already has a personality, which presumably can enhance or detract from what you put on top of it.

That simple fact provides the premise for this book. The sauce and topping recipes on the following pages are specifically designed to complement the flavored pastas with which they are served—to create pleasing contrasts of flavors, as well as striking harmonious color compositions. In many cases tastes, textures, and combinations are deliberately bolder than you might expect from a plate of ordinary pasta. Yet, I've taken great pains to ensure that all the recipes are easy to prepare.

Each chapter of the book centers on recipes meant to be served with a single commonly available type of pasta that you might find in your local stores. Though I've begun each particular chapter with a recipe for the kind of pasta featured, you needn't feel you have to make that pasta yourself from scratch; chances are, a brief shopping expedition will turn up the flavored pasta in question or one of the other pasta options I offer for each recipe. In fact, don't let a lack of flavored pasta deter you from trying a recipe that sounds good: Virtually all of the dishes in this book will taste delicious with your favorite plain old pasta!

Pasta and Sauce Basics

Making and Cooking Fresh Flavored Pasta

The following instructions for making fresh pasta require only a hand-cranked (or electrically cranked) roller-type pasta machine, the best-known brand of which is the Atlas machine imported from Italy.

To get the intensity of color and flavor required in most vegetable-based pastas, I've employed the simple trick of using pureed baby food vegetables, which are remarkably high in quality and purity, blend well with the other ingredients, and save you the time and fuss of pureeing.

Mix the dough as directed in the recipes at the beginning of each chapter. Use your eyes and fingertips to help you achieve the desired consistency, and be patient; you'll soon get the hang of it. Then use the following procedure for kneading and cutting it.

Kneading the Pasta Dough

On a lightly floured work surface, knead the dough by hand for a minute or two: Use the heel of your hand to press the dough down and away from you; then fold it over and give the dough a quarter turn. If it feels sticky, sprinkle with a little flour. Once sufficiently kneaded, the dough will feel smooth, firm, and elastic, without a trace of stickiness.

With a large knife, cut the ball of dough into four equal pieces. Flatten

1

each piece into a circle slightly smaller than the width of the rollers on your pasta maker. Lightly flour the circle on both sides.

Rolling the Dough

With the rollers set to the widest width, crank a circle through the machine, turning the crank smoothly and steadily. Fold the dough in half, give it a quarter turn, dust both sides with flour, and crank it through again. Repeat until the dough rolls through in a smooth, elastic, fairly dry sheet.

Decrease the roller width by one setting. Lightly dust both sides of the fully kneaded sheet of pasta with flour and crank it through the machine, which will flatten and elongate it. Continue dusting and cranking the sheet of pasta at ever-narrower settings until the desired width of pasta is reached—a sheet about $\frac{1}{32}$ inch thick, which corresponds to the "5" setting on Atlas machines. The resulting pasta should feel soft, smooth, dry, and supple.

Repeat the kneading and rolling process with the remaining pieces of dough.

Drying the Pasta Dough

As you finish rolling out each sheet of dough, hang it to dry on a flour-dusted pasta rack or a flour-dusted broomstick supported between two chairs. Within about 20 minutes, the pasta will feel noticeably drier while still remaining pliant. If you wish to speed the drying process, blow the pasta with a hand-held electric hair dryer on its lowest setting. Don't let the sheets of dough get so dry that they lose their flexibility and turn stiff.

Cutting the Pasta Dough

When the pasta dough is dry but still flexible, secure the cutting attachment to the pasta machine. Cut each long strip of pasta into more manageable lengths of 1 to 2 feet. One piece at a time, crank the pasta through the cutting mechanism. Gather up the resulting ribbons of pasta into small, fist-sized nests and place on a floured dish towel or plate until you are ready to cook them.

A Note on Pasta Shapes

Your choice of the width to which you will cut your fresh pasta depends to some extent on the sauce or topping with which you plan to serve it: More robust sauces call for wider, more robust noodles, while delicate dishes complement fine strands of pasta. But, ultimately, there's no hard and fast rule, and you should feel free to serve your pasta cut to whatever width you fancy.

A roller-type pasta machine will typically cut pasta into one of two different widths: fettuccine or tagliatelle, about ¼ inch wide; and thin strands of angel hair no more than 1/16 inch wide. If you wish to experiment with wider shapes, such as 1-inch-wide papardelle or ½-inch-wide fettucci, lightly roll up sheets of pasta like a jelly roll and cut them crosswise to the desired width with a sharp knife.

Storing Fresh Pasta

Freshly made pasta that you don't intend to cook right away should be wrapped in an airtight container and refrigerated for up to 1 week; it may also be frozen for up to 3 months.

Cooking and Serving Fresh Pasta

Having a higher water content than dry pasta, fresh pasta cooks fairly quickly.

The 1¼ to 1½ pounds of fresh pasta yielded by each pasta recipe in this book requires about 6 quarts of water for cooking. Bring the water to a boil in a large pot. Scatter in the pasta, taking some care to separate the individual noodles with your fingertips. Boil for 1 to 3 minutes, depending on how dry the pasta was and what size the noodles were cut to. To test for doneness, use a long fork or a slotted spoon to fish out a noodle; blow on it to cool it down, then bite into it. The noodle should be tender but still slightly chewy—*al dente*, as the Italians say.

Drain the pasta well in a colander or strainer and serve immediately.

A Note on Cooking Times

Dried flavored pasta, purchased from the supermarket shelf, will take longer to cook than the pasta you make yourself or the kind you buy from the refrigerated case. For that reason, I have not given specific times for cooking pasta in the individual sauce and topping recipes in this book. Depending on the kind of pasta you begin with, perform a little simple mental arithmetic to determine the correct moment to start cooking your pasta during the preparation of any given recipe.

A Guide to Basic Ingredients and Preparations

We are lucky today to have such a wide selection of high-quality ingredients from around the world available in virtually any local market we venture into. Nearly all of the ingredients in this book may be easily found in the market you frequent, and, for the few exceptions, I've included in the introductory notes to specific recipes suggestions of where you might find special ingredients.

Keeping some specific ingredients on hand in your own kitchen will help streamline your shopping for pasta recipes—as will the few basic preparations detailed here:

Butter. When a recipe calls for butter, I suggest you use unsalted (sweet) butter. Its flavor is finer than salted butter, and it allows you greater leeway in seasoning a recipe to your specific tastes. If you buy butter in quantity, you can store extra sticks in the freezer.

Cheeses. All of the cheeses in this book can be found in the cheese section of a well-stocked market or delicatessen. One cheese worth keeping on hand at all times is a good-quality imported Italian Parmesan. For the best flavor and value for your money, buy it in block form, grating it or shaving it into thin curls with a vegetable peeler as needed.

Chili Peppers. Chili peppers, called for in some recipes in this book, contain oils that can cause a painful burning sensation on contact with eyes or skin. If necessary, use kitchen gloves when handling chilies, particularly if you have any cuts or abrasions or are especially sensitive. After handling, wash your hands liberally with lots of warm, soapy water. Take extra care not to touch your eyes when handling chilies; if you accidentally do so, splash plenty of cool running water in your eyes to rinse them.

Garlic. Whole heads of garlic can keep for weeks or longer if stored in a well-ventilated, dry place. To peel a garlic clove easily, place it on a work surface and cover with the side of a broad-bladed knife; carefully but firmly hit your fist or the heel of your hand down on top of the knife, taking care to avoid the edge. The clove will crush slightly, loosening the skin.

Herbs. Most good food stores and greengrocers now carry a wide array of fresh herbs, which add an extra dimension of flavor to most of the recipes in this book.

Nuts. Richly flavored and crunchy, toasted nuts make an attractive and delicious garnish for many pasta dishes. To toast nuts, start with plain shelled or blanched nutmeats that have not already been roasted, salted, or otherwise cooked or seasoned. Preheat the oven to 325°F. Spread the nuts in a single layer on a baking sheet and bake just until light golden brown: no more than 3 to 5 minutes for small nuts such as pine nuts or slivered almonds; up to 10 minutes for larger, whole nuts. Check frequently to safeguard against burning. The nuts will go on cooking and darkening in color for a few minutes after you remove them from the oven. Once the nuts are cool, store them in an airtight container.

Olive Oil. Olive oil's rich, fruity flavor and aroma lend great character to pasta dishes. Extra-virgin olive oil is preferable. Extracted from olives on the first pressing without use of heat or chemicals, it has the greatest, purest aroma and flavor. Store olive oil in its airtight container, away from light and heat.

Peppers. Oven roasting develops an intense flavor and tender texture in bell and chili peppers. To roast them, put them on a baking sheet in the middle of a 500°F oven. Roast until their skins are evenly blistered and blackened, about 25 minutes, turning them occasionally so they roast evenly. Remove the baking sheet from the oven and cover the peppers with a kitchen towel. When they are cool enough to handle, carefully pull out the stems, peel away the blackened skins, open up the peppers, and remove the seeds, using a teaspoon to pick up any strays. Some recipes call for the juices inside the roasted pepper to be saved for extra flavor.

Salt and Pepper. Salt is so much an issue of personal taste and diet these days that I've made extra efforts not to specify salt quantities in most of the recipes in this book. Instead, recipe instructions call for seasoning to taste. As for its constant companion, pepper, I recommend using a hand-turned mill to get freshly ground black pepper, which has the maximum flavor and aroma. While you can also buy whole white (that is, hulled) peppercorns to grind fresh, white pepper has a milder flavor to begin with—so I don't specify freshly ground white pepper in the recipes where it is used, wanting to save home cooks the inconvenience of constantly swapping black and white peppercorns in their home pepper grinders.

Shrimp. Fresh shrimp are easily peeled before cooking: Just use your thumbs to split open their shells between the legs and pull the thin, flexible shell away. Shrimp also benefit from *deveining*—a word that actually describes removing the gray-black, veinlike intestinal tract. To do so, use a small, sharp knife to make a shallow slit where you see the vein along the shrimp's convex side; then pull out the vein with your fingers, or lift it out with the tip of the knife.

Tomato Concentrate. Throughout the book, I call for double-strength tomato concentrate, an Italian import widely available in 4½-ounce tubes. Twice as strong as and even more flavorful than canned tomato paste, it also keeps better in the refrigerator, thanks to the twist-on cap that reseals the tube. If you can't find the concentrate, substitute twice the amount of regular canned tomato paste.

Tomatoes, Canned. Keep a good supply on hand of canned tomatoes, either whole or crushed, in their own juice with no added seasonings; avoid already-seasoned products, which leave you less choice of how to flavor the dishes you cook.

Tomatoes, Fresh. Except in the height of summer, when fresh tomatoes are at their sun-ripened best, I always use plum-shaped Roma tomatoes, which have a consistently acceptable flavor and texture. To peel a tomato, use a small, sharp knife to cut out its core and to slit a shallow X in the skin at the opposite end. Submerge the tomato in boiling water for about 20 seconds, then remove it with a slotted spoon and submerge in cold water. From the X, peel away the skin with your fingertips or the blade of a small knife. To seed the tomato, cut it in half and squeeze gently to force out the seed sacs.

A Note on Cooking Times

No two stoves are alike, and therefore no two stoves will cook the same dish in exactly the same length of time. Cooking times given in the recipes in this book are therefore approximate. More important are the sensory cues given in each recipe. Use your eyes, nose, tongue, and fingertips to help you judge when food is properly done.

Beet Pasta

Beet Pasta

Bay Shrimp Sauté with Lemon Butter and Dill

Spinach Pesto with Lemon-Dill Grilled Chicken

Ground Chicken with Carrots in Lemon-Dill Cream Sauce

Grilled Chicken, Ricotta, and Arugula

Smoked Gouda Cream and Baby Peas

Crème Fraîche, Parmesan, and Chives

Beet Pasta

❦

This pasta has a distinctive edge of sweetness from the pureed beets that also give it a bright, rosy color. You can also include 1 to 2 tablespoons of grated lemon zest for beet-lemon pasta.

> **2 to 3 cups all-purpose flour**
> **½ cup pureed beets baby food**
> **3 extra-large eggs**
> **½ teaspoon salt**
> **1 to 2 tablespoons heavy cream**

Put 2½ cups of the flour along with the beets, eggs, and salt in a food processor fitted with the metal blade. Process just until they form a ball of smooth dough that rides around the bowl on the blade, about 1 minute. If the dough seems too sticky, sprinkle in a little of the flour and pulse it in; if it seems too dry and does not form a ball, drizzle in a little of the cream.

Turn the dough out onto a floured work surface and continue as directed in the pasta-making instructions detailed in "Pasta and Sauce Basics."

Makes 1¼ to 1½ pounds fresh pasta; 4–6 servings

Bay Shrimp Sauté
with Lemon Butter and Dill

❊

The sweetness and ruby color of beet pasta finds subtle partnership in tiny bay shrimp, which are sold precooked in the seafood departments of good-sized food stores. The lemon butter and fresh dill are natural complements to both beets and shrimp.

> **1 cup (2 sticks) unsalted butter, cut
>   into pieces**
> **2 medium shallots, finely chopped**
> **1 pound peeled bay shrimp, precooked**
> **2 tablespoons fresh lemon juice**
> **2 tablespoons finely grated fresh
>   lemon zest**
> **2 tablespoons finely chopped fresh dill**

In a large skillet or saucepan, melt the butter over moderate heat. Add the shallots and sauté until tender, 2 to 3 minutes.

Add the shrimp, lemon juice, and zest and cook just until the shrimp are heated through, 1 to 2 minutes more.

Toss the shrimp and lemon butter with cooked pasta and garnish with the dill.

Serves 4–6

Spinach Pesto with
Lemon-Dill Grilled Chicken

❧

Using fresh spinach to replace the basil usually featured in pesto produces a sauce with an edge of astringency that nicely complements the hint of sweetness in beet pasta. Thin strips of marinated grilled chicken breast look—and taste—beautiful on top. For the best flavor and texture, use the smallest baby spinach leaves you can find; or at the very least take care to strip the tough, stringy stems and ribs from larger leaves. Wash the spinach thoroughly to remove all traces of sand, then dry the leaves with a kitchen towel to remove all drops of moisture. Try this topping on lemon or tomato pasta, too.

1 pound boneless, skinless
   chicken breasts
1¼ cups extra-virgin olive oil
2 tablespoons fresh lemon juice
2 tablespoons finely chopped fresh dill
Salt
Freshly ground black pepper
2 medium garlic cloves
1½ cups packed stemmed baby spinach
   leaves, thoroughly washed
1 cup freshly grated Parmesan cheese
1 cup pine nuts, toasted (see Index)

Put the chicken breasts between two sheets of plastic wrap and, using a heavy rolling pin, flatten them to a uniform thickness.

In a mixing bowl, stir together 2 tablespoons of the oil with the lemon juice and dill; turn the chicken breasts in the mixture and leave to marinate at room temperature 15 to 30 minutes.

Meanwhile, preheat the grill or broiler until very hot. Season the chicken breasts with salt and pepper and grill or broil until golden, about 5 minutes per side.

When the chicken is almost done, put the garlic in a food processor fitted with the metal blade; pulse the machine until the garlic is finely chopped. Add the spinach, Parmesan, and pine nuts; pulse until coarsely chopped. Add the remaining oil and process until the mixture forms a smooth paste, stopping once or twice to scrape down the bowl. If the pesto seems too thick, pulse in a little hot water.

When the chicken is done, cut it crosswise into ½-inch-wide strips. Toss the pesto with cooked pasta and top with the chicken.

Serves 4–6

Ground Chicken with Carrots in Lemon-Dill Cream Sauce

❀

A splash of cream enriches this thick ground-chicken topping, enhanced by lemon and dill—two time-honored companions to both chicken and the beets that flavor the pasta. Try this also with spinach, tomato, carrot, or bell pepper pasta.

¼ cup (½ stick) unsalted butter,
   cut into pieces
2 medium-to-large shallots,
   finely chopped
1½ pounds ground chicken
6 tablespoons fresh lemon juice
1½ cups heavy cream
½ cup chicken broth
2 bay leaves
¼ cup finely chopped fresh dill
2 medium carrots, trimmed and
   cut into ¼- to ½-inch dice
Salt
White pepper
2 tablespoons finely chopped fresh
   Italian parsley

In a medium-to-large saucepan or skillet, melt the butter over moderate heat. Add the shallots and sauté until tender, 2 to 3 minutes. Add the ground chicken and sauté, breaking up the chicken into fine bits with a wooden spoon, until it has lost its pink color and left a brown glaze on the pan, about 10 minutes.

Add the lemon juice, raise the heat slightly, and stir and scrape the bottom of the pan with the wooden spoon to dissolve the pan deposits. When the lemon juice has almost evaporated, stir in the cream, broth, bay leaves, and dill and gently boil until thick but still fairly liquid, 12 to 15 minutes, adding the carrots halfway through the cooking time.

Remove and discard the bay leaves. Season to taste with salt and white pepper and serve over cooked pasta, garnishing with the parsley.

Serves 4–6

Grilled Chicken, Ricotta, and Arugula

❈

Quickly grilled or broiled chicken here is cut into robust chunks and tossed with rosy-pink beet pasta and ricotta cheese; whole baby arugula leaves add a dash of green and a slight bitterness to counterbalance the sweetness in the other ingredients.

¼ cup extra-virgin olive oil	¾ cup (1½ sticks) unsalted butter, cut
¼ cup fresh lemon juice	into pieces
1 pound boneless, skinless	1 pound fresh ricotta cheese, at
chicken breasts	room temperature
Salt	2 cups packed baby arugula leaves
Freshly ground black pepper	½ cup freshly grated Parmesan cheese

In a mixing bowl, stir together the oil and lemon juice; turn the chicken breasts in the mixture and leave to marinate at room temperature 15 to 30 minutes.

Meanwhile, preheat the grill or broiler until very hot. Season the chicken breasts with salt and pepper and grill or broil until golden, 5 to 7 minutes per side.

After turning the chicken, melt the butter in a medium saucepan over moderate heat. As soon as the chicken is done, pour the butter over cooked pasta in a mixing bowl and toss well. Cut the chicken into ½- to 1-inch chunks and add the chunks along with the ricotta, dropped by hand in small clumps, to the pasta. Add the arugula and Parmesan and toss gently. Pass salt and pepper for guests to season to taste.

Serves 4–6

Smoked Gouda Cream and Baby Peas

❊

Widely available in well-stocked food store cheese departments, smoked Gouda cheese has a richness and sweet smokiness that stand up well to the distinctive flavor of beet pasta. The peas add a vibrant touch of contrasting color and flavor. If you're in a bind for fresh peas, you can substitute frozen petits pois. Try serving this with red bell pepper or tomato pasta, too.

1 cup shelled baby peas
¼ cup (½ stick) unsalted butter
2 medium shallots, finely chopped
2½ cups heavy cream

1 pound smoked Gouda cheese, shredded
1 tablespoon finely chopped fresh Italian parsley

Bring a small saucepan of lightly salted water to a boil. Add the peas and cook just until tender. Drain and set aside, keeping the peas warm.

In a medium saucepan, melt the butter over moderate heat. Add the shallots and sauté until tender, about 2 minutes.

Add the cream; when it is hot but before it starts to boil, stir in the smoked Gouda cheese. Raise the heat slightly as it begins to melt. Bring to a boil, stirring constantly. Reduce the heat and simmer gently until thick and creamy, about 5 minutes.

Toss the sauce with cooked pasta and scatter the peas on top. Garnish with the parsley.

Serves 4–6

Crème Fraîche, Parmesan, and Chives

❧

A French-style cultured cream product with the richness and consistency of lightly whipped heavy cream and an edge of tang reminiscent of sour cream, crème fraîche provides just the right subtle complement to beet pasta. It is available with increasing frequency in quality food stores and delicatessens. You could use, if you wish, mascarpone, a similar Italian product. The simple topping also goes well with carrot or lemon pasta.

1½ cups crème fraîche
1 cup freshly grated Parmesan cheese
Freshly ground black pepper
¼ cup finely chopped fresh chives

Put the crème fraîche in a small saucepan. Stirring constantly, warm it over low-to-moderate heat, just until heated through.

Toss the warm crème fraîche with cooked pasta and sprinkle generously with Parmesan. Season to taste with black pepper. Garnish with the chives.

Serves 4–6

Bell Pepper Pasta

Bell Pepper Pasta

Sautéed Shrimp and Mushrooms in Green Peppercorn Cream

Seared Tuna and Hot Asian Vinaigrette with Pickled Ginger

Rustic Anchovy-Olive Tapenade with Tuna and Parmesan Shavings

Crabmeat with Chinese Mustard Cream, Plum Sauce, Scallions,
and Cilantro

Lobster Tail with Parmesan Cream, Caviar, Basil, and Pine Nuts

Chicken Huntsman Style

Grilled Beef with Baby Vegetable Sauté

Grilled Veal with Dijon Mustard Cream

Melted Ricotta, Fresh Herbs, Butter, and Garlic

Alfredo with Prosciutto

Chinese-Style Minced Chicken

Bell Pepper Pasta

❦

You can choose to make this pasta with red, yellow, or green bell peppers. Add 1 or 2 tablespoons of chopped fresh basil or oregano, if you like.

> **1 medium bell pepper, roasted, peeled,**
> **stemmed, and seeded (see Index),**
> **juices reserved**
> **2 to 3 cups all-purpose flour**
> **3 extra-large eggs**
> **½ teaspoon salt**
> **1 to 2 tablespoons heavy cream**

Put the pepper and juices in a food processor fitted with the metal blade and process until smoothly pureed, stopping several times to scrape down the bowl.

Add 2½ cups of the flour and the eggs and salt and process just until they form a ball of smooth dough that rides around the bowl on the blade, about 1 minute. If the dough seems too sticky, sprinkle in a little of the flour and pulse it in; if it seems too dry and does not form a ball, drizzle in a little of the cream.

Turn the dough out onto a floured work surface and continue as directed in the pasta-making instructions detailed in "Pasta and Sauce Basics."

Makes 1¼ to 1½ pounds fresh pasta; 4–6 servings

Sautéed Shrimp and Mushrooms in Green Peppercorn Cream

❧

Use the smallest, freshest raw shrimp you can find for this rich and savory sauce, which also goes well with spinach, lemon, or squid ink pasta.

6 tablespoons unsalted butter
½ pound button mushrooms,
   cut into ¼-inch-thick slices
4 medium shallots, finely chopped
1½ tablespoons green peppercorns,
   coarsely crushed
3 cups heavy cream
1 cup fish stock
1 cup dry white wine

2 tablespoons finely chopped fresh
   Italian parsley
2 bay leaves
1½ pounds small fresh shrimp, peeled
   and deveined
Salt
White pepper
Fresh dill sprigs, for garnish

In a large skillet or saucepan, melt the butter over moderate heat. Add the mushrooms, shallots, and peppercorns and sauté until the shallots are tender, 2 to 3 minutes.

Add the cream, fish stock, white wine, parsley, and bay leaves, raise the heat, and boil briskly until the sauce is fairly thick and reduced by about half, 15 to 20 minutes.

Stir in the shrimp, reduce the heat slightly, and simmer gently until the shrimp are cooked through, about 5 minutes. Remove the bay leaves. Season the sauce to taste with salt and white pepper and toss with cooked pasta. Garnish with the dill sprigs.

Serves 4–6

Seared Tuna and Hot Asian Vinaigrette with Pickled Ginger

❦

Think of this, if you like, as a sort of hot main-course pasta salad. Buy the best-quality fresh ahi tuna available from your local seafood market, having them cut it into the number of portions you plan to serve. All the other ingredients should be available in a well-stocked food store or Asian market.

½ cup rice vinegar
2 tablespoons soy sauce
2 teaspoons sugar
1 teaspoon wasabi powder
   (Japanese green horseradish)
¼ cup Asian sesame oil
1½ pounds fresh ahi tuna fillet, cut
   into individual serving portions
Salt
Freshly ground black pepper
½ cup peanut oil
2 medium shallots, finely chopped
6 tablespoons thinly sliced pink
   pickled gingerroot
2 tablespoons coarsely
   chopped cilantro
1 large scallion, cut diagonally into
   thin slices

Stir together the vinegar, soy sauce, sugar, and wasabi powder.
Put about 2 tablespoons of the mixture in a shallow bowl and drizzle in

1 tablespoon of the sesame oil. Turn the tuna in the mixture and leave to marinate at room temperature for 30 minutes.

While the tuna marinates, preheat the grill or broiler until very hot. When the 30 minutes are up, season the tuna with salt and pepper and grill or broil close to the heat until well seared but still pink inside, 2 to 3 minutes per side.

While the tuna cooks, heat the peanut oil in a large skillet or wok. Add the shallots and sauté about 1 minute. Taking care to avoid splattering, stir in the remaining vinegar mixture. When it begins to simmer, stir in the remaining sesame oil. Season to taste with salt and pepper.

Toss cooked pasta with the hot dressing and place individual portions on plates or in bowls. Top with the tuna. Garnish with the pickled ginger, cilantro, and scallion.

Serves 4–6

Rustic Anchovy-Olive Tapenade with Tuna and Parmesan Shavings

❦

A popular Provençale dip or spread, tapenade combines many of the region's most robust ingredients: black olives, anchovies, garlic, capers, and olive oil. This version adds pine nuts for extra substance and chops the mixture to a coarse texture—rather than the traditional smooth paste—to form a quickly tossed sauce for bell pepper pasta topped with chunks of canned tuna and shavings of Parmesan cheese. Also good with spinach or tomato pasta.

4 medium garlic cloves
1 cup extra-virgin olive oil
¾ pound cured Niçoise or Kalamata
   black olives, pitted (about 1½ cups)
½ cup packed fresh Italian
   parsley leaves
⅓ cup pine nuts, toasted (see Index)
¼ cup coarsely chopped fresh chives

¼ cup drained capers
¼ cup fresh lemon juice
2 2-ounce tins anchovy fillets, drained
2 6½-ounce cans tuna in oil, drained
   and coarsely flaked
¼ pound block Parmesan cheese,
   shaved into thin curls (see Index)

Put the garlic in a food processor fitted with the metal blade and pulse until coarsely chopped. Add the olive oil, olives, parsley, pine nuts, chives, capers, lemon juice, and anchovies. Pulse the machine on and off until the mixture forms a coarse puree in which individual pieces are still visible, stopping occasionally to scrape down the bowl.

Toss the tapenade with cooked pasta and top with the tuna and Parmesan shavings. Serve immediately.

Serves 4–6

Bell Pepper Pasta

Crabmeat with Chinese Mustard Cream, Plum Sauce, Scallions, and Cilantro

❀

This intensely flavored sauce gains subtle fire from the inclusion of a dab of hot Chinese mustard, available in well-stocked food stores and Asian markets. Plum sauce adds a contrasting touch of sweetness. Serve with squid ink pasta, too.

2 tablespoons unsalted butter
2 medium shallots, finely chopped
3 cups heavy cream
1 tablespoon rice vinegar
2 teaspoons prepared Chinese or
   English mustard
1¼ pounds flaked cooked crabmeat,
   picked free of any shell or cartilage

¼ cup bottled Chinese plum sauce
2 medium scallions, cut diagonally
   into thin slices
3 tablespoons coarsely chopped
   cilantro leaves

In a saucepan or skillet, melt the butter over moderate heat. Add the shallots and sauté until tender, 2 to 3 minutes. Add the cream, bring to a boil, and simmer briskly until reduced by about a third, 7 to 10 minutes.

Stir together the rice vinegar and mustard and stir it into the cream. Stir in the crabmeat and continue cooking until heated through, 1 to 2 minutes more.

Toss the sauce with cooked pasta and place individual portions on plates or in bowls. Drizzle with the plum sauce and garnish with the scallions and cilantro.

Serves 4–6

Bell Pepper Pasta

Lobster Tail with Parmesan Cream, Caviar, Basil, and Pine Nuts

❦

When you want something really luxurious, pull out the checkbook and head to your best local food store to shop for the ingredients for this recipe. Most good seafood markets or departments will sell fresh or frozen lobster tails; Australian rock lobster tails seem to be reliably available. Since the caviar is a garnish rather than a featured item, you can use the less expensive domestic product or even golden caviar (whitefish roe), salmon roe, or lumpfish roe—that is, unless you really want to splurge. Squid ink or spinach pasta makes a good alternative.

1½ pounds lobster tails in the shell
6 tablespoons unsalted butter
4 medium shallots, finely chopped
1 cup dry white wine
1 cup fish stock
2 cups heavy cream
Salt
White pepper
¾ cup freshly grated Parmesan cheese
6 tablespoons finely shredded fresh
  basil leaves
¼ cup caviar
¼ cup pine nuts, toasted (see Index)

Preheat the broiler until very hot.

With the tip of a small, sharp knife, carefully cut lengthwise through the shells along the underside of the lobster tails. With your thumbs, carefully pry apart the shells and peel them away from the meat. Slice the meat crosswise into ½-inch-thick medallions.

In a large skillet or saucepan, melt 4 tablespoons of the butter over moderate heat. Add the shallots and sauté until tender, 2 to 3 minutes. Add the wine and fish stock and bring to a boil; boil briskly until the sauce has reduced by half, 7 to 10 minutes. Stir in the cream and continue boiling until thick and reduced by about a third, about 10 minutes more.

A few minutes before the sauce is done reducing, melt the remaining butter in a small saucepan. Brush the lobster medallions with the butter and season lightly with salt and white pepper. Broil close to the heat until lightly browned and cooked through, 1 to 2 minutes per side.

Stirring constantly, sprinkle the Parmesan into the cream sauce; continue simmering and stirring until it is fully melted. Stir in half the basil. Season to taste with salt and white pepper.

Toss the cream sauce with cooked pasta and place individual portions on plates or in bowls. Arrange the lobster medallions on top and add a dollop of caviar in the center. Garnish with the pine nuts and the remaining basil.

Serves 4–6

Chicken Huntsman Style

❀

The rough-and-ready Italian chicken stew known as cacciatore *is transformed here into a quick sauté for red bell pepper pasta. You can also serve it over spinach, herb, or carrot pasta.*

¼ cup extra-virgin olive oil

4 medium shallots, finely chopped

4 strips smoked bacon,
  coarsely chopped

1 small green bell pepper, stemmed,
  seeded, and cut into ½-inch squares

1 small onion, coarsely chopped

2 ounces mushrooms, cut into
  ½-inch pieces

1 pound boneless, skinless
  chicken breasts, cut crosswise
  into ½-inch-wide strips

½ cup dry red wine

1 28-ounce can whole tomatoes,
  including liquid

2 medium carrots, cut into ½-inch dice

2 tablespoons coarsely chopped fresh
  Italian parsley

1 tablespoon double-concentrate
  tomato paste

2 teaspoons sugar

2 teaspoons dried oregano

2 bay leaves

3 tablespoons thinly shredded fresh
  basil leaves

In a large skillet or saucepan, heat half the oil over high heat. Add the shallots, bacon, bell pepper, onion, and mushrooms; sauté until tender and just beginning to brown, 3 to 5 minutes. Remove the vegetables and set aside.

Heat the remaining oil over high heat, add the chicken, and sauté until it just begins to turn golden, 2 to 3 minutes.

Add the wine and stir and scrape to deglaze the skillet. Add the tomatoes, breaking them up with your hands. Stir in the carrots, parsley, tomato paste, sugar, oregano, bay leaves, and vegetables that were set aside. Simmer until the sauce is thick but still slightly liquid, about 20 minutes. Remove the bay leaves.

Spoon the sauce over cooked pasta and toss gently. Garnish with the basil.

Serves 4–6

Grilled Beef with Baby Vegetable Sauté

❦

A particularly elegant way to serve steak, this treatment also goes very well with tomato, spinach, herb, or carrot pasta.

1½ pounds well-trimmed beef sirloin, top round, or other tender steak, about 1 inch thick
¾ cup extra-virgin olive oil
Salt
Freshly ground black pepper
2 medium shallots, finely chopped
2 medium scallions, cut diagonally into thin slices
¼ pound baby zucchini, trimmed and cut in half lengthwise
¼ pound baby golden squash, trimmed and cut in halves
2 small Japanese eggplants, trimmed and cut diagonally into ¼-inch-thick slices

¼ cup (½ stick) unsalted butter, cut into pieces
¼ pound cherry or baby yellow tomatoes, stemmed and cut in halves
2 tablespoons fresh lemon juice
½ cup freshly grated Parmesan cheese
1 tablespoon finely chopped fresh Italian parsley
1 tablespoon finely chopped fresh chives
1 tablespoon finely shredded fresh basil leaves

Preheat the grill or broiler until very hot.

Lightly brush the steak all over with about 1 tablespoon of the olive oil. Season both sides lightly with salt and generously with black pepper. Grill or broil the steak close to the heat until well charred but still fairly rare inside, about 5 minutes per side.

While the steak is cooking, heat the remaining oil in a large skillet or wok over moderate-to-high heat. Add the shallots and scallions and sauté until tender, 2 to 3 minutes. Add the zucchini, squash, and eggplant and sauté until almost tender-crisp, 3 to 4 minutes more. Add the butter and tomatoes and sauté just until the tomatoes are hot, 1 to 2 minutes more. Sprinkle in the lemon juice and season to taste with salt and pepper.

Toss the vegetable mixture and the Parmesan with cooked pasta and place individual portions on plates or in bowls. Cut the steak crosswise diagonally into ¼-inch-thick slices, saving the juices. Drape the slices on top of the pasta and spoon the juices over them. Garnish with the parsley, chives, and basil.

Serves 4–6

Grilled Veal with Dijon Mustard Cream

❦

Tender little slices of grilled veal make a particularly indulgent topping for red bell pepper pasta—especially when partnered with a rich cream sauce subtly seasoned with Dijon mustard. Try this on tomato, spinach, carrot, or cornmeal pasta, if you like.

¼ cup (½ stick) unsalted butter
2 medium shallots, finely chopped
3 cups heavy cream
1½ tablespoons creamy Dijon mustard
1½ pounds veal tenderloin, trimmed
Salt
White pepper
¼ cup pine nuts, toasted (see Index)
2 tablespoons finely chopped
* fresh chives*
2 tablespoons finely chopped
* fresh basil*

Preheat the grill or broiler.

Meanwhile, in a medium saucepan or skillet, melt the butter over moderate heat. Pour off and reserve half the butter.

Add the shallots to the remaining butter in the pan and sauté 1 to 2 minutes. Add 2½ cups of the cream; stir together the remaining cream with the mustard and add to the pan. Bring to a boil, then reduce the heat slightly and simmer briskly, stirring occasionally, until reduced by about half to coating consistency, 15 to 20 minutes.

About 10 minutes before the sauce is reduced, brush the veal with the reserved melted butter and season with salt and white pepper. Grill or broil until golden brown and done medium, about 5 minutes per side.

Season the sauce to taste with salt and white pepper and gently toss with cooked pasta. Place individual portions on plates or in bowls. Cut the veal diagonally into ¼-inch-thick slices and drape them on top. Sprinkle with the pine nuts and garnish with the chives and basil.

Serves 4–6

Melted Ricotta, Fresh Herbs, Butter, and Garlic

&

The sweet, mild, creamy flavor of snowy white fresh ricotta cheese complements the sweetness and bright color of red bell pepper pasta. Try this with tomato, lemon, or even squid ink pasta, too.

1 cup (2 sticks) unsalted butter, cut into pieces
4 medium garlic cloves, finely chopped
2 pounds fresh ricotta cheese, at room temperature, drained
Salt
White pepper
2 tablespoons finely chopped fresh Italian parsley
2 tablespoons finely chopped fresh chives
2 tablespoons finely chopped fresh basil

In a large skillet, melt the butter over low heat. Add the garlic and sauté until tender, 1 to 2 minutes.

With your fingers, quickly crumble the ricotta in walnut-sized clumps into the skillet. Season with salt and white pepper and sprinkle in half the parsley, chives, and basil.

When the ricotta has half melted but still retains the shape of its individual clumps, less than a minute, gently toss the sauce with freshly cooked pasta. Garnish with the remaining herbs.

Serves 4–6

Alfredo with Prosciutto

✿

The classic pasta sauce originated in Rome's Alfredo alla Scrofa restaurant gains an enticing embellishment from thin strips of the intensely flavored ham from Parma, Italy—the better to highlight the sweetness of red bell pepper pasta. Try it with tomato, spinach, lemon, or cornmeal pasta, as well.

¾ cup (1½ sticks) unsalted butter, cut
    into pieces
½ pound thinly sliced prosciutto,
    cut into ¼- by 1-inch strips
1½ cups heavy cream
1½ cups freshly grated
    Parmesan cheese
Freshly ground black pepper
2 tablespoons finely chopped
    fresh chives

In a medium saucepan, melt the butter over low heat. Add the prosciutto and sauté about 1 minute, stirring with a wooden spoon to keep the strips from clumping together.

Stir in the cream and raise to moderate heat. When the cream is hot, gradually sprinkle and stir in the Parmesan. As soon as the cheese has melted and thickened the sauce, season generously to taste with pepper and toss the sauce with cooked pasta. Garnish with the chives.

Serves 4–6

Chinese-Style Minced Chicken

❀

A mixture of bottled black-bean sauce, sesame oil, soy sauce, and dried shiitake mushrooms—all available in Asian markets and well-stocked food stores—contribute rich texture and flavor to this topping based on ground chicken. It also goes well with carrot, lemon, or spinach pasta.

¼ cup peanut oil

2 medium garlic cloves,
  finely chopped

1 large scallion, thinly sliced

1 tablespoon finely grated
  fresh gingerroot

1¼ pounds ground chicken

8 dried shiitake mushrooms, soaked
  in warm water until soft, rinsed
  well, stems trimmed off and
  discarded, and caps finely chopped

1 cup bottled Chinese
  black-bean sauce

2 tablespoons hot chili oil

2 tablespoons rice vinegar

2 tablespoons soy sauce

1 tablespoon Asian toasted sesame oil

2 teaspoons light brown sugar

Salt

White pepper

2 tablespoons finely chopped cilantro

In a large wok or skillet, heat the peanut oil over moderate-to-high heat. Add the garlic, scallion, and ginger and stir-fry for 1 minute. Add the chicken and mushrooms and stir-fry, breaking up the chicken into fine pieces, just until it begins to brown, 5 to 7 minutes.

Add the black-bean sauce, chili oil, rice vinegar, soy sauce, sesame oil, and sugar. Simmer, stirring, until the mixture is thick, 2 to 3 minutes more. Season to taste with salt and white pepper.

Spoon over cooked pasta and garnish with the cilantro.

Serves 4–6

Carrot Pasta

Carrot Pasta

Pork, Red Wine, and Mushroom Ragout

Sweet-and-Sour Chicken

Printanier with Roma Tomatoes

Gruyère Cheese Sauce with Cauliflower and Caraway Seeds

Brown Butter, Parsley, and Parmesan

Carrot Pasta

❦

Pureed carrots give this pasta a bright orange hue and characteristic hint of sweetness. Add 1 to 2 tablespoons of chopped fresh dill or grated orange zest to the dough, if you wish.

2 to 3 cups all-purpose flour
½ cup pureed carrots baby food
3 extra-large eggs
½ teaspoon salt
1 to 2 tablespoons heavy cream

Put 2½ cups of the flour along with the carrots, eggs, and salt in a food processor fitted with the metal blade. Process just until they form a ball of smooth dough that rides around the bowl on the blade, about 1 minute. If the dough seems too sticky, sprinkle in a little flour and pulse it in; if it seems too dry, drizzle in a little of the cream.

Turn the dough out onto a floured work surface and continue as directed in the pasta-making instructions detailed in "Pasta and Sauce Basics."

Makes 1¼ to 1½ pounds fresh pasta; 4–6 servings

Pork, Red Wine, and Mushroom Ragout

❧

Orange zest adds just a hint of sweetness to this sauce, enhancing its affinity with carrot pasta. Try it with bell pepper or beet pasta, too.

6 tablespoons unsalted butter, cut
    into pieces
2 medium onions, finely chopped
½ pound button mushrooms, cut into
    ¼-inch-thick slices
1 pound ground pork
1½ cups beef broth
1 cup dry red wine
1 teaspoon dried rosemary
2 bay leaves

3 tablespoons double-concentrate
    tomato paste
1 teaspoon sugar
2 tablespoons finely grated fresh
    orange zest
Salt
Freshly ground black pepper
2 tablespoons finely chopped fresh
    Italian parsley
1 tablespoon finely chopped fresh dill

In a large skillet, melt the butter over moderate heat. Add the onions and mushrooms; sauté until the onions are tender, 3 to 5 minutes. Add the pork and sauté, breaking it up with a wooden spoon, until it just begins to brown, 7 to 10 minutes.

Add the broth and red wine and bring to a boil, stirring and scraping the bottom of the skillet with a wooden spoon to dissolve pan deposits. Stir in the rosemary, bay leaves, tomato paste, and sugar; simmer until thick, about 10 minutes. Stir in the orange zest and season to taste with salt and pepper. Remove the bay leaves.

Toss gently with cooked pasta and garnish with the parsley and dill.

Serves 4–6

Carrot Pasta

Sweet-and-Sour Chicken

❦

There's no rule that says Chinese dishes must be served over rice; in fact, some regions of China serve more dishes over noodles. This contemporized version of sweet-and-sour chicken goes very well with carrot, spinach, squid ink, or bell pepper pasta.

6 tablespoons vegetable oil

2 tablespoons cornstarch

1½ pounds boneless, skinless chicken breasts, cut crosswise into ¼-inch-thick strips

2 medium garlic cloves, finely chopped

1½ tablespoons finely grated fresh gingerroot

1 medium red onion, quartered and cut into ½-inch slices

1 medium red bell pepper, halved, stemmed, seeded, and cut into ½-inch squares

1 medium celery stalk, cut crosswise into ¼-inch-wide slices

2 large Roma tomatoes, cored and cut into ½-inch chunks

⅔ cup coarsely chopped fresh or drained canned pineapple

½ cup frozen baby peas

¾ cup chicken broth

¼ cup light brown sugar

¼ cup fresh lemon juice

2 tablespoons soy sauce

2 tablespoons coarsely chopped cilantro leaves

Heat half the oil in a wok or skillet over high heat. While it heats, put the cornstarch in a small fine-mesh sieve and tap it over the chicken pieces to dust them lightly and evenly.

When the oil is hot, add the chicken pieces and stir-fry until they begin to turn golden, 3 to 5 minutes. Remove from the wok with a slotted spoon and set aside.

Add the remaining oil to the wok with the garlic and ginger; when they sizzle, add the red onion, bell pepper, and celery, stir-frying about 2 minutes. Add the tomatoes, pineapple, and peas and stir-fry 1 minute more. Add the broth, sugar, lemon juice, and soy sauce and stir until the sugar dissolves, scraping the wok to dissolve the deposits on its surface. Add the chicken pieces and simmer until the liquid thickens to coating consistency, 2 to 3 minutes more.

Gently toss the mixture with cooked pasta and garnish with the cilantro.

Serves 4–6

Printanier with Roma Tomatoes

❦

A rapid sauté of fresh green springtime vegetables and Roma tomatoes enlivens carrot pasta. The topping is also good with tomato, herb, lemon, or cornmeal pasta.

¾ cup extra-virgin olive oil

4 medium shallots, finely chopped

½ pound thin asparagus, trimmed, tips left whole, spears cut diagonally into ¼-inch-thick slices

½ pound small zucchini, trimmed and cut diagonally into ¼-inch-thick slices

¼ pound small button mushrooms, trimmed, left whole or halved

1 small green or red bell pepper, quartered, stemmed, and seeded, quarters cut crosswise into ¼-inch-wide slices

6 large Roma tomatoes, cored and coarsely chopped

¼ cup (½ stick) unsalted butter, cut into pieces

Salt

Freshly ground black pepper

2 tablespoons finely chopped fresh Italian parsley

2 tablespoons thinly shredded fresh basil

Freshly grated Parmesan cheese

Heat the oil in a large skillet over high heat. Add the shallots and sauté about 1 minute.

Add the asparagus, zucchini, mushrooms, and bell pepper and sauté until barely tender-crisp, 4 to 5 minutes. Add the tomatoes and butter and continue sautéing until the tomatoes begin to soften and give up their juice, 2 to 3 minutes more. Season to taste with salt and pepper.

Gently toss the vegetable mixture, parsley, and basil with cooked pasta and pass the Parmesan for guests to add to taste.

Serves 4–6

Carrot Pasta

Gruyère Cheese Sauce with Cauliflower and Caraway Seeds

❀

Precooking the cauliflower in milk—whole or low-fat—reduces much of its assertiveness, helping it harmonize with the cheese sauce and the edge of spice from the caraway seeds. The subtle, creamy colors and rich, slightly sweet flavors look and taste marvelous with carrot pasta, as well as red bell pepper, cornmeal, herb, or spinach pasta.

2 cups whole or low-fat milk	*1 tablespoon caraway seeds*
1 small head cauliflower, separated into bite-sized florets	*2½ cups heavy cream*
	1 pound Gruyère cheese, shredded
¼ cup (½ stick) unsalted butter	*1 tablespoon finely chopped fresh*
2 medium shallots, finely chopped	*Italian parsley*

In a medium saucepan, bring the milk to a boil. Add the cauliflower, reduce the heat, and simmer until the florets are barely tender-crisp, 4 to 5 minutes. Drain, discarding the milk; set the cauliflower aside.

Rinse out the saucepan. Melt the butter over moderate heat and add the shallots and caraway seeds; sauté about 2 minutes.

Add the cream; when it is hot but before it starts to boil, stir in the Gruyère cheese. Raise the heat slightly as it begins to melt. Bring to a boil, stirring constantly. Reduce the heat and simmer gently until the mixture is thick and creamy, about 5 minutes.

Return the cauliflower to the pan and simmer to heat it through, about 1 minute more. Gently toss the cauliflower and sauce with cooked pasta, garnish with the parsley, and serve immediately.

Serves 4–6

Brown Butter, Parsley, and Parmesan

❀

Here carrot pasta gets a variation of the same simple, classic treatment given to garden-fresh carrots. Substitute fresh dill for part or all of the parsley, if you like. This treatment is also good with beet or lemon pasta.

> **1 cup (2 sticks) unsalted butter, cut**
> **into pieces**
> **½ cup coarsely chopped fresh Italian**
> **parsley leaves**
> **1½ cups freshly grated Parmesan**
> **cheese**
> **Salt**
> **Freshly ground black pepper**

In a medium skillet, melt the butter over moderate heat. When the butter begins to foam, add the parsley and continue cooking until the butter begins to turn a nut-brown color, about 1 minute more.

Pour the butter-parsley mixture over cooked pasta, add the Parmesan, season to taste with salt and pepper, and toss gently.

Serves 4–6

Cornmeal Pasta

Cornmeal Pasta

Sautéed Swiss Chard and Sun-Dried Tomatoes

Grilled Red Chili-Dusted Salmon with Mild Green Chili Pesto

Grilled Shrimp with Avocado-Cilantro Pesto

Fajita-Style Chicken, Hot Chili Peppers, and Red Onion

New Mexican Green Chili with Pork

Fresh Green and Red Chilies con Queso

Grilled Pork Tenderloin with Apples and Honey-Mustard Cream

Chili-Dusted Romano Cream with Bacon and Pine Nuts

Cornmeal Pasta

❧

Use your choice of yellow or blue cornmeal for this rich, earthy-tasting pasta. The cornmeal, which has a coarser texture than flour, may make this dough a bit more difficult to work with. If you like, try adding ½ to 1 tablespoon pure red chili powder, mild or hot.

¾ cup cornmeal
1¾ to 2¼ cups all-purpose flour
3 extra-large eggs
½ teaspoon salt
1 to 2 tablespoons heavy cream

Put the cornmeal in a food processor fitted with the metal blade and process for about 1 minute. Add 1½ cups of the flour and the eggs and salt and process just until they form a ball of smooth dough that rides around the bowl on the blade, about 1 minute. If the dough seems too sticky, sprinkle in a little of the flour and pulse it in; if it seems too dry and does not form a ball, drizzle in a little of the cream.

Turn the dough out onto a floured work surface and continue as directed in the pasta-making instructions detailed in "Pasta and Sauce Basics."

Makes 1¼ to 1½ pounds fresh pasta; 4–6 servings

Sautéed Swiss Chard and Sun-Dried Tomatoes

❈

Swiss chard's fresh flavor combines gentle hints of bitterness and sweetness that show off the earthy sweetness of cornmeal pasta. The tangy sun-dried tomatoes add their own bright color and taste. This sauce also goes well with fresh herb, spinach, or carrot pasta.

8 large leaves Swiss chard, trimmed
1 cup (2 sticks) unsalted butter, cut into pieces
4 medium shallots, finely chopped
¾ cup sun-dried tomato pieces, cut into ¼-inch-wide strips

¾ cup heavy cream
Salt
White pepper
½ cup freshly grated Parmesan cheese

With a sharp knife, cut the dark green leafy parts of the Swiss chard from the white stems. Stack the dark green parts, bunch them up, and cut crosswise into ¼-inch-wide strips. Thinly slice the white stems.

In a large skillet, melt the butter over moderate-to-high heat. Add the shallots and sauté 1 minute. Add the Swiss chard and sun-dried tomatoes and sauté until the greens just begin to wilt, about 2 minutes more.

Stir in the cream and continue cooking, stirring frequently, until the sauce is thick and the pieces of stem are tender-crisp, about 5 minutes more. Season to taste with salt and white pepper.

Gently toss the sauce with cooked pasta. Sprinkle the Parmesan on top.

Serves 4–6

Grilled Red Chili-Dusted Salmon with Mild Green Chili Pesto

❦

The distinctive taste of salmon stands up well to a light dusting of moderately hot chili powder and looks beautiful against a background of green chili pesto and yellow cornmeal pasta. Be sure to use pure powdered red chilies—available in well-stocked food stores and Latino markets—rather than the sort of commercial spice blend intended for chili con carne. This goes well with tomato, red bell pepper, or squid ink pasta, too.

1½ pounds fresh salmon fillet,
    skin removed
6 tablespoons unsalted butter, melted
Salt
White pepper
2 tablespoons mild-to-moderate pure
    red chili powder
4 medium shallots
8 long mild green (Anaheim or New
    Mexican) chilies, roasted, stemmed,
    seeded, and peeled (see Index)
1¼ cups pine nuts, toasted (see Index)
1 cup freshly grated Parmesan cheese
1 cup extra-virgin olive oil
½ cup packed cilantro leaves
Cilantro sprigs, for garnish

Preheat the grill or broiler.

When the grill or broiler is hot, brush the salmon all over with the butter and season lightly with salt and white pepper. Put the chili powder in a small fine-mesh sieve and shake over the salmon to dust it evenly. Broil close to the heat until golden brown, about 3 minutes per side.

While the salmon is cooking, prepare the pesto. Put the shallots in a food processor fitted with the metal blade. Pulse the machine until the shallots are coarsely chopped, stopping to scrape down the bowl if necessary.

Add the green chilies, 1 cup of the pine nuts, the Parmesan, olive oil, and cilantro leaves. Process until uniformly pureed but still slightly coarse in texture, stopping as necessary to scrape down the bowl. Taste and adjust the seasonings.

Gently toss the pesto with cooked pasta and place individual portions in bowls or on plates. Cut the salmon into the number of portions being served and place on top. Garnish with the remaining pine nuts and the cilantro sprigs.

Serves 4–6

Grilled Shrimp with
Avocado-Cilantro Pesto

❦

A cross between the Mexican avocado dip known as guacamole and an Italian-style pesto, the sauce makes a dazzling canvas for grilled marinated shrimp; and both sauce and shrimp go very well with cornmeal pasta, as well as tomato or red bell pepper pasta. Be sure to make the pesto just before serving; if left to stand, it could begin to discolor.

> **2 teaspoons medium-to-hot paprika**
> **¼ cup fresh lemon juice**
> **18 large shrimp (about 1⅓ pounds),**
>   **peeled and deveined, tails left on**
> **½ cup heavy cream**
> **2 medium garlic cloves**
> **1 medium Haas avocado, peeled**
>   **and pitted**
> **½ cup plus 2 tablespoons pine nuts,**
>   **toasted (see Index)**
> **½ cup Parmesan cheese**
> **¼ cup packed cilantro leaves**
> **Salt**
> **White pepper**
> **Cilantro sprigs, for garnish**

In a mixing bowl, stir together the paprika and half of the lemon juice. Add the shrimp, toss well, and leave to marinate at room temperature for about 30 minutes.

Preheat the broiler.

Start to warm the cream in a medium saucepan or skillet over low-to-moderate heat.

While the cream is warming, put the garlic in a food processor fitted with the metal blade and pulse until coarsely chopped. Add the avocado, ½ cup of the pine nuts, the Parmesan, cilantro leaves, and the remaining lemon juice and puree, stopping a few times to scrape down the bowl as necessary.

Season the shrimp with salt and white pepper and broil 4 to 5 inches from the heat until golden on the outside but still juicy within, 1 to 2 minutes per side.

While the shrimp is broiling, stir the avocado mixture into the cream and continue stirring until the sauce is heated through. Taste and adjust the seasoning with salt and white pepper.

Gently toss the sauce with cooked pasta and place individual portions on plates or in bowls. Top with the grilled shrimp. Garnish with the remaining pine nuts and the cilantro sprigs.

Serves 4–6

Fajita-Style Chicken, Hot Chili Peppers, and Red Onion

❧

Instead of being folded in hot tortillas as it normally would be, this variation on the popular southwestern dish of seared chicken strips is served atop cornmeal pasta. It's also good with spinach, tomato, lemon, or saffron pasta.

¼ cup extra-virgin olive oil
1½ pounds boneless, skinless chicken breasts, cut crosswise into ¼-inch-wide strips
Salt
Freshly ground black pepper
4 medium garlic cloves, finely chopped
2 fresh green serrano chilies, halved, stemmed, seeded (see Index), and cut crosswise into thin strips
2 fresh long green mild (Anaheim or New Mexico) chilies, halved, stemmed, seeded (see Index), and cut crosswise into ¼-inch-wide strips

2 medium red bell peppers, quartered, stemmed, seeded, and cut crosswise into ¼-inch-wide strips
1 medium red onion, quartered and cut crosswise into ¼-inch-wide slices
1½ cups chicken broth
1 pound Roma tomatoes, coarsely chopped
1 tablespoon dried oregano
2 tablespoons lime juice
6 ounces feta cheese, crumbled
2 tablespoons finely chopped cilantro leaves

In a large skillet over high heat, heat the olive oil. Lightly season the chicken with salt and pepper and sauté until golden brown, about 5 minutes. With a slotted spoon, remove the chicken and set aside. Pour off about half the oil.

Reduce the heat to medium and sauté the garlic about 30 seconds. Add the chilies, bell peppers, and onion and sauté about 2 minutes more.

Add the chicken broth, tomatoes, and oregano; raise the heat and bring to a boil. Reduce the heat to low, add the chicken, and simmer, stirring frequently, until the liquid in the pan thickens, 10 to 12 minutes more. Stir in the lime juice and season to taste with salt and pepper.

Lightly toss the chicken mixture with cooked pasta and place individual portions on plates or in bowls. Sprinkle with the feta and garnish with the cilantro.

Serves 4–6

New Mexican Green Chili with Pork

❀

Cornmeal pasta becomes an avant-garde tortilla for this version of New Mexico's traditional green chili stew. Try the sauce, too, with tomato or red bell pepper pasta.

¼ cup vegetable oil
¾ pound lean pork tenderloin, cut
　　into ½-inch cubes
2 medium garlic cloves, finely chopped
12 long mild green (Anaheim or
　　New Mexican) chilies, roasted,
　　stemmed, and peeled (see Index),
　　but not seeded, finely chopped

1 teaspoon dried oregano
1 to 2 cups water
Salt
White pepper
¼ pound dry, crumbly feta cheese
2 tablespoons finely chopped cilantro

In a skillet over moderate heat, heat the oil. Add the pork and sauté until browned, 4 to 5 minutes. Remove the pork with a slotted spoon. Set aside. Pour off and discard all but 2 tablespoons of fat from the skillet.

Return the skillet to the heat and add the garlic. As soon as the garlic sizzles, add the chilies, oregano, and reserved pork. Stir in enough of the water to keep the mixture fairly liquid and the pork submerged. Reduce the heat and simmer gently, adding more water as necessary to maintain a thick but fluid consistency, for about 30 minutes, until the pork is tender. Season to taste with salt and white pepper.

Gently toss the sauce with cooked pasta. Crumble the feta cheese over each serving and garnish with the cilantro.

Serves 4–6

Fresh Green and Red Chilies con Queso

❦

One of Mexico's most indulgent appetizers, the cheese-and-chili-pepper melt known as chili con queso, *is ideally suited to cornmeal pasta. Fresh red and green chili peppers can be found in well-stocked markets or Latino food stores; if no red ones are available use green jalapeño or serrano chilies. The sauce is also good with tomato or spinach pasta.*

¼ cup (½ stick) unsalted butter
1 long mild green (Anaheim or
    New Mexican) chili, roasted,
    stemmed, and peeled (see Index),
    but not seeded, finely chopped
1 red or green jalapeño chili,
    stemmed, seeded, and finely
    chopped (see Index)
1 red or green serrano chili, stemmed,
    seeded, and finely chopped (see
    Index)

3 cups heavy cream
1 pound Monterey Jack cheese,
    shredded
½ pound sharp cheddar cheese,
    shredded
2 tablespoons finely chopped cilantro

In a medium saucepan over moderate heat, melt the butter. Add the chilies and sauté until they begin to turn tender, 3 to 4 minutes.

Add the cream and, as soon as it is hot but before it starts to boil, stir in the Monterey Jack and cheddar cheeses. Raise the heat slightly as they begin to melt. Bring the sauce to a boil, stirring constantly. Reduce the heat and simmer gently until the sauce is thick and creamy, about 5 minutes. Gently toss with cooked pasta and serve immediately, garnished with cilantro.

Serves 4–6

Cornmeal Pasta

Grilled Pork Tenderloin with Apples and Honey-Mustard Cream

❀

Pork, apples, honey, mustard, walnuts, and corn all just go together, combining earthiness and sweetness in each of their distinctive flavors. This topping would also go well with bell pepper pasta.

¼ cup (½ stick) unsalted butter
3 medium shallots, finely chopped
3 cups heavy cream
1½ tablespoons grainy mustard
1½ tablespoons honey, at room
   temperature
1 crisp green apple
1½ pounds pork tenderloin, trimmed
Salt
Freshly ground black pepper
¼ cup walnut pieces, toasted
   (see Index)
3 tablespoons finely chopped
   fresh chives

Preheat the grill or broiler.

Meanwhile, in a medium saucepan or skillet melt the butter over moderate heat. Pour off and reserve half the butter.

Add the shallots to the remaining butter in the pan and sauté 1 to 2 minutes. Add 2½ cups of the cream; stir together the remaining cream with the mustard and honey and add to the pan. Bring to a boil, then reduce the heat slightly and simmer briskly, stirring occasionally, until reduced by about half to coating consistency, 15 to 20 minutes.

About 12 minutes before the sauce is reduced, core and peel the apple and cut it into 12 wedges. Brush the pork and apple with the reserved melted butter and season with salt and pepper. Grill or broil the pork and apple slices until golden brown and done medium, about 5 minutes per side for the pork; remove the apple slices earlier if they begin to brown too much.

Toss the sauce with cooked pasta and place individual portions on plates or in bowls. Cut the pork diagonally into ¼-inch-thick slices and drape them on top with the apple slices. Sprinkle with the walnuts and garnish with the chives.

Serves 4–6

Chili-Dusted Romano Cream with Bacon and Pine Nuts

&

The sweet, earthy tastes of cornmeal pasta and a cream sauce flavored with tangy Romano cheese provide a perfect background for crisp, crumbled bacon and crunchy toasted pine nuts. Use pure powdered dried red chilies rather than one of the packaged blends of spices. If you can find New Mexican blue cornmeal, use it for the pasta. The sauce also works well with spinach or red bell pepper pasta.

6 strips smoked bacon
1½ cups heavy cream
1½ cups freshly grated Romano cheese
2 tablespoons pure red chili powder
¼ cup pine nuts, toasted (see Index)
2 tablespoons finely chopped fresh
    Italian parsley

Under the broiler or in a skillet over moderate heat, cook the bacon until crisp and golden brown. Drain on paper towels and set aside.

Put the cream in a medium saucepan over moderate heat. When the cream is hot, gradually sprinkle and stir in the Romano cheese. As soon as the cheese has melted and thickened the sauce, gently toss the sauce with cooked pasta.

Put the chili powder in a small fine-mesh strainer and tap the strainer over the pasta to dust the sauce with the powder. With your hands, crumble the bacon on top. Garnish with the pine nuts and parsley.

Serves 4-6

Spinach Pasta

Spinach Pasta

Shrimp Scampi with Bell Peppers and Pine Nuts

Spicy Red Clam Sauce

Mushroom Marinara

Ground Chicken with Nutmeg Butter and Hazelnuts

Bolognese alla Marsala

Spicy Tomato Sauté with Melted Goat Cheese

Tomato, Ricotta, and Basil

Melted Blue Cheese with Butter and Pine Nuts

White Wine Cream with Crispy Pancetta and Pine Nuts

Spicy Aglio e Olio

Gorgonzola Cream with Toasted Walnuts

Four Cheeses with Toasted Pine Nuts

Spinach Pasta

❦

One of the classic fresh pastas gets intense color and flavor from pureed spinach. Add a garlic clove, pureed with a garlic press, for an extra dimension.

> **2 to 3 cups all-purpose flour**
> **½ cup pureed spinach baby food**
> **3 extra-large eggs**
> **½ teaspoon salt**
> **1 to 2 tablespoons heavy cream**

Put 2½ cups of the flour along with the spinach, eggs, and salt in a food processor fitted with the metal blade. Process just until they form a ball of smooth dough that rides around the bowl on the blade, about 1 minute. If the dough seems too sticky, sprinkle in a little of the flour and pulse it in; if it seems too dry and does not form a ball, drizzle in a little of the cream.

Turn the dough out onto a floured work surface and continue as directed in the pasta-making instructions detailed in "Pasta and Sauce Basics."

Makes 1¼ to 1½ pounds fresh pasta; 4–6 servings

Shrimp Scampi with Bell Peppers and Pine Nuts

❀

A mixture of red and yellow pepper strips looks best against the green spinach fettuccine. The topping also works with squid ink or tomato pasta; but for the latter, substitute green bell peppers for the red called for here to maintain a contrast of color.

½ cup extra-virgin olive oil

½ cup (1 stick) unsalted butter

4 medium garlic cloves, finely chopped

1 pound medium shrimp, shelled and deveined

1 large red bell pepper, roasted, peeled, stemmed, seeded (see Index), and torn into ¼- to ½-inch-wide strips, juices reserved

1 large yellow bell pepper, roasted, peeled, stemmed, seeded (see Index), and torn into ¼- to ½-inch-wide strips, juices reserved

Salt

White pepper

6 tablespoons pine nuts, toasted (see Index)

2 ounces Parmesan cheese, shaved into thin curls (see Index)

Heat the oil and butter with the garlic in a large skillet over moderate-to-high heat. As soon as the garlic sizzles, add the shrimp and sauté just until they turn pink, about 1 minute. Reduce the heat, add the peppers and their juices, and sauté until the shrimp are done and the peppers are heated through, about 1 minute more. Season to taste with salt and white pepper.

Arrange the shrimp and peppers on top of cooked pasta and drizzle evenly with the liquid from the skillet. Scatter the pine nuts and Parmesan curls on top and serve immediately.

Serves 4–6

Spicy Red Clam Sauce

❀

There is nothing timid about this version of a classic red clam sauce given a decidedly Latin-American twist for spinach pasta. Canned baby clams make preparation easy. Be sure to use pure red chili powder, available in well-stocked food stores and Latino markets. Squid ink pasta stands up well to this sauce, too.

¼ cup extra-virgin olive oil
4 medium garlic cloves,
  finely chopped
2 medium shallots, finely chopped
1 medium green bell pepper, stemmed,
  seeded, and cut into ¼-inch dice
1 fresh jalapeño chili, stemmed,
  seeded, and finely chopped
  (see Index)
1 tablespoon medium-to-hot
  red chili powder

1 28-ounce can whole tomatoes,
  including liquid
1 tablespoon double-concentrate
  tomato paste
1 tablespoon dried oregano
2 teaspoons sugar
2 bay leaves
¾ pound shelled baby clams, drained
Salt
Freshly ground black pepper
¼ cup finely chopped cilantro

In a large skillet or saucepan, heat the olive oil over moderate heat. Add the garlic, shallots, bell pepper, and jalapeño; sauté until barely tender, about 2 minutes. Sprinkle in the chili powder and sauté about 1 minute more, stirring to break up any lumps of chili powder.

Add the tomatoes, breaking them up with your hands. Stir in the tomato paste, oregano, sugar, and bay leaves. Bring to a boil, reduce heat, and simmer until thick, 15 to 20 minutes. Stir in the clams and simmer 2 to 3 minutes more. Season to taste with salt and pepper. Just before serving over cooked pasta, remove the bay leaves and stir in the cilantro.

Serves 4–6

Spinach Pasta

Mushroom Marinara

❦

An abundance of sliced fresh mushrooms raises this version of the classic tomato sauce above the everyday, creating a great vegetarian topping for fresh spinach pasta. The sauce is also good with carrot, green bell pepper, cornmeal, herb, or lemon pasta.

¼ cup extra-virgin olive oil
2 medium garlic cloves, finely chopped
1 medium onion, finely chopped
1 pound fresh mushrooms, trimmed and cut into ¼-inch-thick slices
1 28-ounce can whole tomatoes, including liquid
2 tablespoons double-concentrate tomato paste
2 bay leaves

¼ cup finely chopped fresh basil
2 tablespoons finely chopped fresh Italian parsley
1 tablespoon sugar
2 teaspoons dried oregano
1 teaspoon dried rosemary
Salt
Freshly ground black pepper
Freshly grated Parmesan cheese

In a large skillet or saucepan, heat the oil over moderate heat. Add the garlic and onion and sauté until tender, 2 to 3 minutes.

Add the mushrooms, raise the heat slightly, and sauté until their edges just begin to turn golden, 5 to 7 minutes.

Add the tomatoes, breaking them up with your hands. Stir in the tomato paste, bay leaves, basil, parsley, sugar, oregano, and rosemary. Gently boil until thick, 15 to 20 minutes. Season to taste with salt and pepper. Remove the bay leaves.

Gently toss with cooked pasta, passing the Parmesan for guests to add.

Serves 4–6

Ground Chicken with Nutmeg Butter and Hazelnuts

❧

There's something comfortingly old-fashioned about this quick sauté of ground chicken breast. The hint of nutmeg is a traditional treatment for spinach. Try this, too, with lemon, fresh herb, or carrot pasta.

½ cup (1 stick) unsalted butter,
  cut into pieces
2 medium shallots, finely chopped
⅛ teaspoon ground nutmeg
1½ pounds ground chicken
½ cup medium-dry white wine
½ cup chicken broth

Salt
White pepper
¼ cup coarsely chopped hazelnuts,
  toasted (see Index)
2 tablespoons finely chopped fresh
  chives

In a large saucepan or skillet, melt half the butter over moderate heat. Add the shallots and nutmeg and sauté until tender, 2 to 3 minutes. Add the ground chicken and sauté, breaking up the chicken with a wooden spoon, until it has lost its pink color and left a brown glaze on the pan, about 10 minutes.

Add the wine and broth, raise the heat slightly, and stir and scrape the bottom of the pan with the wooden spoon to dissolve the pan deposits. When the liquid has reduced by about half, briskly stir in the remaining butter until it melts. Season to taste with salt and white pepper.

Gently toss the sauce with cooked pasta. Scatter the hazelnuts and chives on top.

Serves 4–6

Bolognese alla Marsala

※

A splash of the amber-colored sweet wine from Sicily adds an extra dimension to this robust version of the classic meat sauce. For a change, try the sauce with green bell pepper or fresh herb pasta.

¼ cup olive oil

4 medium garlic cloves, finely chopped

1 large onion, finely chopped

½ pound sweet fresh Italian sausage, casings split and removed

½ pound lean ground beef

⅓ cup Marsala

1 28-ounce can whole tomatoes, including liquid

2 tablespoons double-concentrate tomato paste

½ tablespoon dried basil

½ tablespoon dried oregano

½ tablespoon dried rosemary

1 teaspoon sugar

Salt

Freshly ground black pepper

In a large skillet or saucepan, heat the oil over moderate heat. Add the garlic and onion and sauté until tender, 2 to 3 minutes.

Add the sausage and beef and raise the heat slightly. Sauté until the meat has lost all its pink color and left a brown glaze on the pan, about 10 minutes. Add the Marsala and stir and scrape the bottom of the pan with a wooden spoon to dissolve the pan deposits.

Add the tomatoes, breaking them up with your hands. Stir in the remaining ingredients (except for the salt and pepper), and gently boil until thick, 15 to 20 minutes. Season to taste with salt and pepper.

Gently toss with cooked pasta.

Serves 4–6

Spicy Tomato Sauté with Melted Goat Cheese

❧

The better to stand up to spinach pasta, a dash of hot red pepper flakes spikes the tomatoes in this sauce, making them more than a match as well for melting dabs of tangy, creamy goat cheese. Give the sauce a try, if you like, with green bell pepper, fresh herb, or cornmeal pasta.

¼ cup extra-virgin olive oil
2 medium garlic cloves, finely
   chopped
1 to 1½ teaspoons red pepper flakes
1½ pounds Roma tomatoes, halved,
   cored, seeded (see Index), and cut
   into ½- to 1-inch chunks
1 teaspoon salt

1 teaspoon sugar
1 pound fresh creamy goat cheese,
   at room temperature
½ cup finely shredded fresh
   basil leaves
¼ cup pine nuts, toasted (see Index)

In a large skillet, heat the olive oil over moderate heat. Add the garlic and red pepper flakes to taste and sauté for about 1 minute. Add the tomatoes, raise the heat, sprinkle with the salt and sugar, and sauté just until the juices begin to thicken, 4 to 5 minutes.

With your fingers, drop the goat cheese in walnut-sized clumps into the skillet. Sprinkle in the basil. When the goat cheese has half melted but still retains the shape of its individual clumps, less than a minute, gently toss the sauce with cooked pasta. Garnish with the pine nuts.

Serves 4–6

Tomato, Ricotta, and Basil

❧

The bright red of ripe Roma tomatoes and the white of ricotta cheese look stunning against the green backdrop of spinach pasta. This is also good with green bell pepper, fresh herb, cornmeal, or squid ink pasta.

> **2 tablespoons extra-virgin olive oil**
> **2 tablespoons unsalted butter**
> **2 medium garlic cloves, finely chopped**
> **1½ pounds Roma tomatoes, halved, cored, seeded (see Index), and cut into ½- to 1-inch chunks**
> **1 teaspoon salt**
> **1 teaspoon sugar**
> **1 pound ricotta cheese, at room temperature, drained**
> **½ cup finely shredded fresh basil leaves**

In a large skillet, heat the olive oil and butter over moderate heat. When the butter has melted, add the garlic and sauté for about 1 minute. Add the tomatoes, raise the heat, sprinkle with the salt and sugar, and sauté just until the juices begin to thicken, 4 to 5 minutes.

With your fingers, quickly crumble the ricotta in walnut-sized clumps into the skillet. Sprinkle in half the basil. When the ricotta has half melted but still retains the shape of its individual clumps, less than a minute, gently toss the sauce with cooked pasta. Garnish with the remaining basil.

Serves 4–6

Spinach Pasta

Melted Blue Cheese with Butter and Pine Nuts

❀

The rich results belie the speed with which this topping is prepared. Use whatever good-quality blue-veined cheese is available, but make sure it is one that, though creamy, will crumble fairly easily. Substitute coarsely chopped toasted hazelnuts for the pine nuts, if you wish. Try with bell pepper, cornmeal, or tomato pasta, too.

> **¾ cup (1½ sticks) unsalted butter**
> **¾ pound blue cheese, coarsely crumbled**
> **½ cup pine nuts, toasted (see Index)**

In a medium saucepan or skillet, melt the butter over moderate heat. Sprinkle in the blue cheese and, as soon as it begins to melt slightly, gently toss the butter and cheese with cooked pasta. Garnish with the pine nuts.

Serves 4–6

White Wine Cream with Crispy Pancetta and Pine Nuts

❀

In the absence of the Italian bacon known as pancetta, which is available from well-stocked market delicatessen counters and Italian delis, use the best-quality lean bacon you can find. The sauce is also good with tomato, bell pepper, cornmeal, or herb pasta.

¼ cup (½ stick) unsalted butter, cut into pieces	2 cups heavy cream
2 medium shallots, finely chopped	Salt
¼ pound thinly sliced pancetta, cut into ¼- to ½-inch pieces	White pepper
1 cup medium-dry white wine	⅓ cup pine nuts, toasted (see Index)
	Freshly grated Parmesan cheese

In a large skillet over moderate heat, melt the butter. Add the shallots and pancetta and sauté until the pancetta is golden brown and crisp, 3 to 5 minutes. Remove the pancetta with a slotted spoon and transfer to paper towels. Pour off most of the fat from the skillet.

Add the white wine and stir and scrape over moderate heat to deglaze the skillet. Raise the heat and boil the wine until reduced by about half, 5 to 7 minutes. Stir in the cream and continue boiling until the sauce is thick, about 10 minutes more. Season to taste with salt and white pepper.

Gently toss the sauce with cooked pasta. Scatter the pancetta and pine nuts on top and pass the Parmesan for guests to add to taste.

Serves 4–6

Spicy Aglio e Olio

❦

Garlic browned in olive oil makes one of the simplest of pasta sauces. This version goes one better with the addition of red pepper flakes, which enliven the taste and add a dash of color to a plate of spinach pasta. The sauce also goes well with tomato, bell pepper, or fresh herb pasta.

> **1½ cups olive oil**
> **8 medium garlic cloves, finely**
> **chopped**
> **1½ teaspoons red pepper flakes**
> **Freshly grated Parmesan cheese**

Heat the oil in a large skillet over moderate-to-high heat. Add the garlic and sauté about 1 minute. Sprinkle in the red pepper flakes and continue sautéing until the garlic is golden brown, 1 to 2 minutes more.

Immediately pour the sauce over cooked pasta and toss gently. Pass the Parmesan for guests to sprinkle on to taste.

Serves 4–6

Gorgonzola Cream with Toasted Walnuts

❧

Gorgonzola rates among the tangiest and richest of the world's blue-veined cheeses. If you can't find it in a good food store or Italian deli, substitute the best blue cheese variety available. The sauce's rich, sharp flavor offsets the refreshing astringency of fresh spinach pasta, and its flecks of blue look lovely against the green. Toasted walnuts, earthy and crunchy, add a great contrast of flavor and texture; toasted hazelnut halves would also be good. You can also try the sauce with tomato, bell pepper, or fresh herb pasta.

1 tablespoon butter
1 medium shallot, finely chopped
3 cups heavy cream
1¾ pounds Gorgonzola cheese, crumbled

1 cup shelled walnuts, toasted (see Index)
2 tablespoons finely chopped fresh chives

In a medium saucepan, melt the butter over moderate heat. Add the shallot and sauté until tender, about 2 minutes.

Add the cream, raise the heat slightly, and bring to a boil. Reduce the heat to a simmer and add the crumbled Gorgonzola. Stir continuously until the sauce is thick and the cheese has melted.

Gently toss the sauce with cooked pasta and strew with the walnuts. Garnish with the chives.

Serves 4–6

Four Cheeses
with Toasted Pine Nuts

❧

Rich and complex enough to stand up to the pronounced flavor of spinach, a creamy blend of four cheeses has become one of the classic sauces for this kind of pasta. Feel free to experiment by substituting different kinds of cheese or garnishing with other types of nuts. The sauce also goes well with tomato, bell pepper, or fresh herb pasta.

> *2½ cups heavy cream*
> *¼ pound Gruyère cheese, shredded*
> *¼ pound fontina cheese, shredded*
> *¼ pound Monterey Jack cheese,*
>   *shredded*
> *½ cup freshly grated Parmesan cheese*
> *½ cup pine nuts, toasted (see Index)*
> *2 tablespoons finely shredded fresh*
>   *basil leaves*

Put the cream in a medium saucepan over moderate heat. As soon as the cream is hot, but before it starts to boil, stir in the Gruyère, fontina, and Monterey Jack cheeses.

Raise the heat slightly as the cheeses begin to melt; sprinkle and stir in the Parmesan. Bring to a boil, stirring constantly. Reduce the heat and simmer gently until thick and creamy, about 5 minutes.

Gently toss with cooked pasta, scatter the pine nuts on top, and garnish with the basil.

Serves 4–6

Tomato Pasta

Tomato Pasta

Spicy Shrimp and Roasted Peppers

Grilled Lemon-Rosemary Shrimp with Cannellini Beans and Shallots

Grilled Chicken with Goat Cheese Cream Sauce, Peas, and Peppers

Chicken and Asparagus Sauté with Lemon Butter and Fresh Herbs

Duck and White Wine Ragout

Sirloin Meatballs with Black Pepper Butter and Parmesan

Veal and Eggplant Oreganato

Roasted Bell Pepper and Exotic Mushroom Medley

Sweet Italian Sausage and Pepper Sauté

Sugar Snap Pea Sauté with Lemon Zest

Rustic Pesto with Balsamic Vinegar

Feta Cream with Black Olives and Pine Nuts

Wild Mushroom Parmesan Cream Sauce

Tomato Pasta

❀

Using double-concentrate tomato paste adds further intensity to the color and flavor of this fresh pasta dough. You can also include 1 to 2 tablespoons chopped fresh basil or oregano for tomato-herb pasta.

2 to 3 cups all-purpose flour
½ cup double-concentrate tomato paste
3 extra-large eggs
½ teaspoon salt
1 to 2 tablespoons heavy cream

Put 2½ cups of the flour along with the tomato paste, eggs, and salt in a food processor fitted with the metal blade. Process just until they form a ball of smooth dough that rides around the bowl on the blade, about 1 minute. If the dough seems too sticky, sprinkle in a little of the flour and pulse it in; if it seems too dry and does not form a ball, drizzle in a little of the cream.

Turn the dough out onto a floured work surface and continue as directed in the pasta-making instructions detailed in "Pasta and Sauce Basics."

Makes 1¼ to 1½ pounds fresh pasta; 4–6 servings

Spicy Shrimp
and Roasted Peppers

❀

A few simple but distinctive ingredients show off the vividness of fresh tomato pasta. If you like, you can serve the topping with lemon, cornmeal, spinach, or herb pasta, too.

¾ cup (1½ sticks) unsalted butter,
  cut into pieces
4 medium shallots, finely chopped
2 teaspoons crushed red pepper flakes
1 pound medium shrimp, peeled
  and deveined
1 medium green bell pepper,
  roasted, peeled, stemmed, seeded
  (see Index), and torn into thin
  strips, juices reserved
1 medium red bell pepper,
  roasted, peeled, stemmed, seeded

(see Index), and torn into thin
  strips, juices reserved
1 medium yellow bell pepper,
  roasted, peeled, stemmed, seeded
  (see Index), and torn into thin
  strips, juices reserved
Salt
Freshly ground black pepper
2 tablespoons finely chopped fresh
  Italian parsley
Freshly grated Parmesan cheese

In a large skillet, melt the butter over moderate-to-high heat. As soon as it foams, add the shallots and red pepper flakes and sauté about 1 minute.

Add the shrimp and sauté until they turn uniformly pink, 2 to 3 minutes. Add the roasted peppers and their juices and sauté until heated through, 1 to 2 minutes more.

Season to taste with salt and pepper and toss gently with cooked pasta. Garnish with the parsley and pass the Parmesan for guests to add to taste.

Serves 4–6

Grilled Lemon-Rosemary Shrimp with Cannellini Beans and Shallots

❀

This simple recipe transforms a favorite Italian appetizer into an elegant topping for fresh tomato pasta and is equally good with spinach, herb, or bell pepper pasta. Using already-cooked canned cannellini beans, available in well-stocked food stores and Italian delis, cuts preparation time dramatically. Try substituting an equal weight of fresh tuna fillets for the shrimp.

1¼ cups extra-virgin olive oil
⅔ cup fresh lemon juice
2 tablespoons finely chopped fresh
    rosemary leaves, or 1 tablespoon
    dried rosemary
18 large shrimp (about 1⅓ pounds),
    peeled and deveined, tails left on
4 medium shallots, finely chopped
2 14½-ounce cans cannellini
    (white kidney) beans, rinsed
    and drained

Salt
White pepper
2 tablespoons finely chopped fresh
    Italian parsley
2 tablespoons finely chopped
    fresh chives
4 to 6 small fresh rosemary sprigs
    (optional garnish)

In a mixing bowl, stir together ¼ cup of the olive oil, 2 tablespoons of the lemon juice, and half the rosemary. Add the shrimp and leave to marinate at room temperature for about 30 minutes.

Preheat the broiler.

In a large skillet or saucepan, heat the remaining oil over low-to-moderate heat. Add the shallots and sauté just until they turn translucent, 2 to 3 minutes. Then add the beans and the remaining lemon juice and rosemary and cook until the beans are heated through, about 5 minutes.

Meanwhile, season the shrimp with salt and white pepper and broil 4 to 5 inches from the heat until golden on the outside but still juicy within, 1 to 2 minutes per side.

Season the beans to taste with the salt and white pepper and spoon them and their liquid over cooked pasta; toss gently. Top with the broiled shrimp and garnish with the parsley, chives, and rosemary sprigs.

Serves 4-6

Grilled Chicken with Goat Cheese Cream Sauce, Peas, and Peppers

❧

The now-classic California combination of chicken and goat cheese gains an added dimension from fresh peas and strips of roasted bell pepper. Try this topping with carrot, herb, or lemon pasta, too.

3 tablespoons unsalted butter
1 pound boneless, skinless
   chicken breasts
Salt
White pepper
2 medium shallots, finely chopped
1 cup heavy cream
½ pound creamy fresh goat cheese
¾ pound fresh peas, shelled and
   parboiled for 2 to 3 minutes
   until barely tender
Ground nutmeg
2 yellow or green bell peppers,
   roasted, peeled, stemmed, seeded
   (see Index), and cut into thin strips
2 tablespoons finely chopped
   fresh chives

Preheat the grill or broiler.

In a large skillet, melt the butter over low heat. Brush the chicken breasts with about 2 tablespoons of the butter and season them with salt and white pepper. Grill or broil them until golden, about 7 minutes per side.

As soon as you have turned the chicken, add the shallots to the remaining butter in the skillet. Sauté until tender, 1 to 2 minutes. Add the cream, raise the heat to moderate, and then add the goat cheese, stirring until it melts. Stir in the peas and cook about 1 minute more. Season to taste with salt and white pepper and just a hint of the nutmeg.

Gently toss the sauce with cooked pasta. Cut the chicken breasts crosswise into ¼-inch-wide strips and arrange attractively on top. Garnish with the bell pepper strips and chives.

Serves 4–6

Chicken and Asparagus Sauté with Lemon Butter and Fresh Herbs

☙

Chicken and asparagus complement each other's delicacy, and the tang of lemon butter heightens the qualities of both. Bell pepper or fresh herb pasta would be good options.

1 cup (2 sticks) unsalted butter, cut into pieces

¼ cup extra-virgin olive oil

2 medium garlic cloves, finely chopped

2 dozen asparagus spears, trimmed and cut diagonally into ¼-inch-thick slices (about 2 cups)

1 pound boneless, skinless chicken breasts, cut crosswise into ½-inch-wide strips

¼ cup fresh lemon juice

Salt

White pepper

1 tablespoon finely grated fresh lemon zest

1 tablespoon finely chopped fresh Italian parsley

1 tablespoon finely chopped fresh basil

1 tablespoon finely chopped fresh chives

1 teaspoon finely chopped fresh tarragon

Tomato Pasta

In a large skillet, melt half the butter with 1 tablespoon of the oil over high heat. Add the garlic and sauté until light golden, about 1 minute. Add the asparagus and sauté until tender-crisp, 4 to 5 minutes more. Empty into a bowl and set aside.

Wipe the skillet clean, add the remaining butter and oil, and melt over moderate heat. Add the chicken pieces and sauté until lightly browned, 3 to 5 minutes. Add the lemon juice and stir and scrape the bottom of the skillet with a wooden spoon to deglaze.

Stir in the reserved asparagus and its melted butter. Season to taste with salt and white pepper and stir in the lemon zest.

Spoon and arrange the chicken, asparagus, and lemon butter over freshly cooked pasta. Toss together the fresh herbs and sprinkle on top.

Serves 4–6

Duck and White Wine Ragout

❀

To counterbalance the richness of the duck meat, this recipe calls for a medium-dry white wine with fresh fruitiness and a hint of sweet spice, such as a gewürztraminer or Riesling. The sauce is also good with bell pepper, spinach, cornmeal, or carrot pasta.

½ cup unsalted butter, cut into pieces
2 tablespoons peanut or corn oil
4 medium shallots, finely chopped
1¼ pounds boneless, skinless
duck breasts, cut crosswise into
¼-inch-thick slices
Salt
White pepper
1 cup medium-dry white wine
½ cup chicken broth
2 medium carrots, cut into ¼-inch dice
2 bay leaves
2 teaspoons dried rosemary
2 tablespoons coarsely chopped fresh
Italian parsley

In a large skillet or saucepan, melt 2 tablespoons of the butter with the oil over moderate heat. Add the shallots and sauté about 1 minute.

Season the duck breasts with salt and white pepper and sauté until they lose their pink color and just begin to brown, 3 to 5 minutes. Add the wine and broth and stir and scrape the bottom of the skillet with a wooden spoon to deglaze. Stir in the carrots, bay leaves, and rosemary.

Bring the liquid to a boil, then reduce to a gentle simmer and cook until the duck is tender and the liquid has reduced by about half, 10 to 15 minutes. Remove the bay leaves and briskly stir in the remaining butter. Season to taste with salt and white pepper.

Gently toss the sauce with cooked pasta and garnish with the parsley.

Serves 4–6

Sirloin Meatballs with Black Pepper Butter and Parmesan

❀

Imagine this topping as a transformation of steak au poivre, the classic black-pepper-crusted steak. Also good with lemon, carrot, or herb pasta.

> **2 large shallots**
> **2 eggs**
> **¾ cup fresh white bread crumbs**
> **½ cup heavy cream**
> **1 teaspoon salt**
> **1 pound ground lean sirloin**
> **1 cup (2 sticks) unsalted butter,**
> ** cut into pieces**
> **Freshly ground black pepper**
> **1 cup freshly grated Parmesan cheese**
> **3 tablespoons finely chopped**
> ** fresh chives**

Preheat the broiler until very hot.

Meanwhile, put the shallots in a food processor fitted with the metal blade and process until finely chopped, stopping if necessary to scrape down the bowl. Add the eggs, bread crumbs, cream, salt, and sirloin and process until well mixed.

Moistening your hands with water, form 1½- to 2-inch meatballs and place them on a broiler tray sprayed with nonstick vegetable oil spray. Broil close to the heat until nicely browned and done medium inside, about 4 minutes per side.

While the meatballs are broiling, melt the butter in a skillet or saucepan over moderate heat. As soon as the butter begins to foam, generously grind in pepper to taste.

Gently toss cooked pasta with the pepper butter and Parmesan. Place the meatballs on top and garnish with the chives.

Serves 4–6

Veal and Eggplant Oreganato

❦

Fresh oregano highlights the sweetness of veal and the earthiness of eggplant in this simple sautéed topping for tomato pasta. If you like, try it on spinach, lemon, or bell pepper pasta.

> **½ cup (1 stick) unsalted butter,**
>   **cut into pieces**
> **¼ cup extra-virgin olive oil**
> **1¼ pounds thin veal scallops, cut**
>   **crosswise into ½-inch-wide strips**
> **Salt**
> **White pepper**
> **1 pound Japanese or small globe**
>   **eggplants, trimmed, peels left on,**
>   **cut into ½-inch chunks**
> **½ cup medium-dry white wine**
> **2 tablespoons finely chopped fresh**
>   **oregano leaves**
> **Fresh oregano sprigs, for garnish**
> **Freshly grated Parmesan cheese**

In a large skillet, melt the butter with the oil over moderate-to-high heat. Lightly season the veal strips with salt and white pepper and sauté until lightly browned, 3 to 5 minutes. Remove from the skillet with a slotted spoon and set aside.

Add the eggplant and sauté until it just begins to brown, 3 to 5 minutes. Add the wine and stir and scrape with a wooden spoon to deglaze the skillet. Stir in the oregano leaves and simmer, stirring frequently, until the eggplant is very tender, about 20 minutes.

Return the veal to the skillet and stir, mashing the eggplant slightly. Cook 1 to 2 minutes more to heat the veal through, then season to taste with salt and white pepper.

Gently toss with cooked pasta and garnish with the oregano sprigs. Pass the Parmesan for guests to add to taste.

Serves 4-6

Roasted Bell Pepper
and Exotic Mushroom Medley

❀

Use whatever fresh exotic mushrooms are available at your local market—porcini, portobello, cremini, shiitake, chanterelle—or, barring that, good, firm domestic mushrooms. Green and yellow bell peppers contrast nicely with the tomato pasta. Try this topping as well with herb, lemon, or spinach pasta.

1 cup extra-virgin olive oil

8 medium garlic cloves, finely chopped

¾ pound porcini, chanterelle, portobello, cremini, or shiitake mushrooms, trimmed and cut into ¼-inch-thick slices

3 medium green bell peppers, roasted, peeled, stemmed, seeded (see Index), and torn into ¼-inch-wide strips

3 medium green bell peppers, roasted, peeled, stemmed, seeded (see Index), and torn into ¼-inch-wide strips

3 medium yellow bell peppers, roasted, peeled, stemmed, seeded (see Index), and torn into ¼-inch-wide strips

2 tablespoons fresh lemon juice

Salt

Freshly ground black pepper

2 tablespoons thinly shredded fresh basil leaves

1 tablespoon finely chopped fresh Italian parsley

Freshly grated Parmesan cheese

In a large skillet, heat the oil over moderate-to-high heat. Add the garlic and sauté 1 minute. Add the mushrooms and sauté until their edges just begin to brown, 3 to 5 minutes.

Add the peppers and sauté until they are heated through, 1 to 2 minutes more. Sprinkle in the lemon juice and season to taste with salt and pepper.

Spoon the vegetables and pan juices over cooked pasta, toss gently, and garnish with the basil and parsley. Pass the Parmesan for guests to sprinkle on to taste.

Serves 4–6

Sweet Italian Sausage
and Pepper Sauté

❦

Fresh, sweet Italian sausages are available in good butcher shops, food stores, and Italian delis. Using lemon and orange juices to deglaze the pan in which the sausage and peppers are sautéed marries the flavors, playing up their inherent sharpness and sweetness. This would also be good with spinach, lemon, or fresh herb pasta.

6 tablespoons extra-virgin olive oil
1 pound sweet Italian sausage, casings split and removed
2 green bell peppers, stemmed, seeded, and thinly sliced
2 yellow bell peppers, stemmed, seeded, and thinly sliced
2 medium garlic cloves, finely chopped
2 tablespoons fresh lemon juice
2 tablespoons orange juice
¼ cup finely chopped fresh Italian parsley
Freshly grated Parmesan cheese

In a large skillet, heat 2 tablespoons of the oil over moderate-to-low heat. Add the sausage and, using a wooden spoon, break it up into coarse chunks. Sauté until the sausage has given up a good deal of its fat but is not yet browned, 3 to 5 minutes. Carefully pour off most of the fat.

Raise the heat to moderate and add the remaining oil. Add the peppers and garlic and sauté until the sausage is golden and the peppers are tender-crisp, 3 to 4 minutes more. Add the lemon and orange juices and stir and scrape to deglaze the skillet; then add the parsley and stir briefly.

Gently toss with cooked pasta and garnish to taste with the Parmesan.

Serves 4–6

Sugar Snap Pea Sauté
with Lemon Zest

❦

The deep green color of sugar snap peas, edible pods and all, looks especially vibrant against the red of tomato pasta, and the tastes and textures are just as complementary. If you can't find sugar snap peas, substitute snow peas. Try this, if you wish, with lemon, bell pepper, or herb pasta as well.

¼ cup extra-virgin olive oil
4 medium shallots, finely chopped
¾ cup (1½ sticks) unsalted butter,
   cut into pieces
1½ pounds fresh sugar snap
   peas, trimmed
1 tablespoon finely grated fresh lemon
   zest
Salt
Freshly ground black pepper
Freshly grated Parmesan cheese

In a large skillet, heat the oil over moderate-to-high heat. Add the shallots and sauté until they just begin to turn golden, 1 to 2 minutes.

Add the butter and, as soon as it melts and begins to foam, add the sugar snap peas and sauté until tender-crisp, 4 to 5 minutes. Sprinkle and stir in the lemon zest.

Toss gently with cooked pasta, passing salt, pepper, and the Parmesan at the table for guests to season their portions to taste.

Serves 4–6

Rustic Pesto
with Balsamic Vinegar

❀

So many of us are used to smooth, creamy pesto sauces that this coarser version comes as a surprise, its color and flavor nicely complementing tomato pasta. A splash of balsamic vinegar adds extra liveliness. Try the sauce as well with red bell pepper pasta.

4 medium garlic cloves
3 cups packed stemmed fresh basil
   leaves
1¼ cups pine nuts, toasted (see Index)
1 cup freshly grated Parmesan cheese
1¼ cups extra-virgin olive oil
2 tablespoons balsamic vinegar
4 to 6 small sprigs fresh basil

Put the garlic in a food processor fitted with the metal blade. Pulse the machine until the garlic is coarsely chopped, stopping to scrape down the bowl if necessary.

Add the basil leaves and 1 cup of the pine nuts and pulse several times until coarsely chopped, stopping to scrape down the bowl. Add the Parmesan and pulse once or twice to incorporate it. Then add the oil and vinegar and pulse just once or twice until all the ingredients are combined, leaving the pesto with a coarse, moist consistency.

Gently toss the pesto with cooked pasta the moment the pasta has been drained. Garnish individual servings with the remaining pine nuts and the basil sprigs.

Serves 4–6

Tomato Pasta

Feta Cream with
Black Olives and Pine Nuts

❦

Between the salty Greek-style goat cheese known as feta and the black olives, you shouldn't need to season this robust sauce with any additional salt. Some fetas tend to be on the dry and crumbly side, so seek out the softest variety available. If you like, add some strips of sun-dried tomato with the olives—a particularly nice contrast if you use this sauce with spinach pasta instead of the tomato pasta.

1 cup heavy cream
¾ pound soft feta cheese
White pepper
¾ cup pitted Kalamata or other
   Mediterranean-style cured
   black olives, pitted and halved
6 tablespoons pine nuts, toasted
   (see Index)

In a medium saucepan or skillet over moderate heat, bring the cream to a bare simmer. Crumble in the feta cheese and stir until it melts. Season to taste with white pepper.

Gently toss the sauce with cooked pasta. Scatter the olives on top and then garnish with the pine nuts.

Serves 4–6

Wild Mushroom
Parmesan Cream Sauce

❧

Dried porcini mushrooms, available year-round in good-quality markets, specialty food stores, and Italian delis, provide the foundation for this richly indulgent sauce that also includes whatever wild mushrooms might be available fresh in your area; a mixture of two or more different wild mushrooms is especially pleasing. In a pinch, use cultivated mushrooms as the fresh component. Try this sauce on spinach, lemon, herb, carrot, or cornmeal pasta, if you like.

1½ ounces dried porcini mushrooms
4 cups heavy cream
6 tablespoons unsalted butter
4 large shallots, finely chopped
2 medium garlic cloves, finely
   chopped
¾ pound fresh chanterelle, oyster,
   portobello, shiitake, or other
   wild mushrooms, stems trimmed,
   caps thinly sliced
½ cup finely grated Parmesan cheese
Salt
White pepper
2 tablespoons finely chopped fresh
   Italian parsley
2 tablespoons finely chopped
   fresh chives

Put the porcini mushrooms in a mixing bowl and add 1 cup of the cream. Leave to soak until soft, about 10 minutes. Pour the porcinis and cream through a very fine-mesh sieve or a strainer lined with cheesecloth; reserve the cream and porcinis and discard any grit or other residue in the strainer. Thinly slice the porcinis.

In a large skillet or saucepan, melt the butter over moderate heat. Add the shallots and garlic and sauté until tender, 2 to 3 minutes. Add the fresh wild mushrooms and the porcinis and sauté about 1 minute more.

Add the reserved cream and the remaining cream, raise the heat slightly, bring to a boil, and simmer until the cream is reduced almost by half, about 15 minutes. Stirring constantly, sprinkle in the Parmesan. Season to taste with a little salt, if necessary, and white pepper.

Gently toss with cooked pasta and garnish with the parsley and chives.

Serves 4–6

Squid Ink Pasta

Squid Ink Pasta

Salmon Caviar and Shallot Butter

Grilled Salmon Medallions with Lemon Zest Marinara and
Fines Herbes

Smoked Salmon with Lemon, Shallots, Pine Nuts, and Herbs

Creamy White Clam Sauce

Creamed Oysters with Jalapeño Salsa Fresca

Seared Sea Scallops with Roasted Pepper and Garlic Cream

Calamari alla Puttanesca Fresca

Crab Cakes and Ginger Cream

Squid Ink Pasta

❦

Ask the best seafood store in your area to save you the ink sacs from freshly cleaned squid; use them to add jet-black color and a subtle taste of the sea to fresh pasta dough.

> **2 to 3 cups all-purpose flour**
> **½ cup fresh squid ink**
> **3 extra-large eggs**
> **½ teaspoon salt**
> **1 to 2 tablespoons heavy cream**

Put 2½ cups of the flour along with the squid ink, eggs, and salt in a food processor fitted with the metal blade. Process just until they form a ball of smooth dough that rides around the bowl on the blade, about 1 minute. If the dough seems too sticky, sprinkle in a little of the flour and pulse it in; if it seems too dry and does not form a ball, drizzle in a little of the cream.

Turn the dough out onto a floured work surface and continue as directed in the pasta-making instructions detailed in "Pasta and Sauce Basics."

Makes 1¼ to 1½ pounds fresh pasta; 4–6 servings

Salmon Caviar and Shallot Butter

❧

Exquisitely simple, this topping features among the most reasonably priced forms of caviar—the large, plump roe of salmon, which possesses the fish's distinctive flavor and looks like rubies against the backdrop of squid ink pasta. You could also try this, if you wish, with golden caviar—domestic whitefish roe. Saffron pasta provides an equally dramatic contrast to the salmon roe.

**1½ cups (3 sticks) unsalted butter,
    cut into pieces
4 small-to-medium shallots, finely
    chopped
½ cup salmon roe
1 tablespoon finely chopped fresh
    basil
1 tablespoon finely chopped fresh
    Italian parsley**

In a small saucepan or skillet, melt the butter over low-to-moderate heat. Add the shallots and sauté until tender, 2 to 3 minutes.

Pour the butter-shallot mixture over individual portions of cooked pasta. Top with dollops of the salmon roe. Toss together the basil and parsley and scatter on top.

Serves 4–6

Grilled Salmon Medallions with Lemon Zest Marinara and Fines Herbes

❦

Adding the bright spark of grated lemon zest and fines herbes—fresh parsley, basil, chives, dill, and tarragon—to a quickly prepared marinara creates a lively background for seared fillets of salmon. This is also excellent with spinach pasta.

6 tablespoons extra-virgin olive oil

2 tablespoons fresh lemon juice

1½ pounds fresh salmon fillet, cut crosswise into 1-inch-thick slices

2 large shallots, finely chopped

2 medium garlic cloves, finely chopped

1 28-ounce can whole tomatoes, including liquid

2 bay leaves

2 tablespoons finely chopped fresh Italian parsley

2 tablespoons finely chopped fresh dill

1 tablespoon finely chopped fresh tarragon leaves

1 tablespoon double-concentrate tomato paste

1 tablespoon sugar

Salt

White pepper

2 tablespoons finely grated fresh lemon zest

2 tablespoons finely shredded fresh basil leaves

2 tablespoons finely chopped fresh chives

In a shallow bowl, stir together 2 tablespoons of the olive oil with the lemon juice. Turn the salmon fillets in the mixture and leave to marinate at room temperature about 30 minutes.

Preheat the broiler. In a medium skillet or saucepan heat the remaining oil over moderate heat. Add the shallots and garlic; sauté until tender, 2 to 3 minutes. Add the tomatoes, breaking them up with your hands. Stir in the bay leaves, parsley, dill tarragon, tomato paste, and sugar. Raise the heat slightly and simmer the sauce until thick, about 15 minutes.

About 7 minutes before the sauce is done, remove the salmon from the marinade and season lightly with salt and white pepper. Broil close to the heat until golden brown, about 3 minutes per side.

Remove the bay leaves from the marinara sauce and stir in the lemon zest. Season to taste with salt and white pepper.

Spoon the sauce over cooked pasta and top with the grilled salmon. Garnish with the basil and chives.

Serves 4–6

Smoked Salmon with Lemon, Shallots, Pine Nuts, and Herbs

&

Each element in this recipe joins the others in luxurious harmony while retaining its own distinctive character. Buy the best-quality Scottish smoked salmon you can find; it's more expensive, but a little goes a long way. Deli-style lox is too fatty for use in this dish. The sauce is also good with saffron, spinach, or fresh basil pasta.

½ cup (1 stick) unsalted butter
¼ cup extra-virgin olive oil
2 medium-to-large shallots, finely chopped
2 tablespoons fresh lemon juice
½ pound thinly sliced smoked salmon, cut crosswise into ¼-inch-wide strips

6 tablespoons freshly grated Parmesan cheese
¼ cup pine nuts, toasted (see Index)
2 tablespoons finely chopped fresh basil
2 tablespoons finely chopped fresh chives
Freshly ground black pepper

In a medium skillet, melt the butter with the olive oil over moderate heat. Add the shallots and sauté 1 to 2 minutes, until translucent. Remove the pan from the heat and quickly stir in the lemon juice.

Pour the hot mixture over cooked pasta and toss with the salmon, Parmesan, pine nuts, basil, and chives. Season to taste with black pepper.

Serves 4–6

Creamy White Clam Sauce

❀

The usual so-called white clam sauce is based largely on white wine and butter. This version, designed to luxuriously complement squid ink pasta, takes the term literally, enriched as it is with cream. The sauce is also good with tomato or spinach pasta.

½ cup (1 stick) unsalted butter,
   cut into pieces
4 medium shallots, finely chopped
1½ cups dry white wine
2 bay leaves
2½ cups heavy cream
1 pound shelled baby clams, drained

Salt
White pepper
¼ cup finely shredded fresh basil
   leaves
2 tablespoons finely chopped fresh
   Italian parsley

In a large skillet or saucepan, heat the butter over moderate heat. Add the shallots and sauté until tender, 2 to 3 minutes.

Add the white wine and bay leaves, raise the heat, and boil until the wine is reduced by about half, 5 to 7 minutes. Add the cream and boil until the liquid has reduced by about a third and is still fluid but fairly thick, 7 to 10 minutes more. Stir in the clams and simmer 2 to 3 minutes more. Remove the bay leaves. Season to taste with salt and white pepper.

Pour over cooked pasta and garnish with the basil and parsley.

Serves 4–6

Creamed Oysters
with Jalapeño Salsa Fresca

❦

Since there's no presentation in the shell, save yourself the trouble and buy the oysters already shucked. The creamy and brightly colored sauce is particularly attractive against a background of squid ink pasta. Try this too with saffron, lemon, or cornmeal pasta.

2 large Roma tomatoes, cored, peeled, halved, seeded (see Index), and cut into ¼-inch dice

1 or 2 jalapeño chilies, roasted, peeled, stemmed, seeded (see Index), and finely chopped

½ medium red onion, finely chopped

¼ cup finely chopped cilantro leaves

2 tablespoons lime juice

Salt

White pepper

½ cup (1 stick) unsalted butter, cut into pieces

4 large shallots, finely chopped

1 quart freshly shucked oysters with their liquor

1½ cups heavy cream

In a bowl, toss together the tomato, jalapeño to taste, red onion, cilantro, and lime juice. Season to taste with salt and white pepper and set aside.

In a medium skillet or saucepan, melt the butter over moderate heat. Add the shallots and sauté until tender, 2 to 3 minutes. Pour the liquor from the oysters into the pan, leaving the oysters behind; raise the heat slightly and simmer briskly until the liquor reduces by about half.

Add the cream, bring to a boil, and boil briskly until the sauce is thick but still fairly liquid, 7 to 10 minutes more. Taste and adjust the seasonings with salt and white pepper.

Reduce the heat to a bare simmer, add the oysters, and poach them until their edges begin to curl, 2 to 3 minutes more.

Spoon the sauce and oysters over individual portions of cooked pasta. Garnish each oyster with a small spoonful of the salsa and serve immediately.

Serves 4–6

Seared Sea Scallops with Roasted Pepper and Garlic Cream

❧

The contrast is stunning: ivory-colored sauce, gold-tinged scallops, and bright red pepper strips, all against a backdrop of black squid ink pasta. Parboiling the garlic cloves in milk before adding them to the cream softens their harsh edge. Try this with tomato, bell pepper, or spinach pasta, too.

> **1 cup milk**
> **4 medium garlic cloves, cut**
> **lengthwise in halves**
> **3 cups heavy cream**
> **24 large sea scallops (about**
> **1⅔ pounds)**
> **¼ cup (½ stick) unsalted**
> **butter, melted**
> **Salt**
> **White pepper**
> **2 medium red bell peppers, roasted,**
> **peeled, stemmed, seeded (see**
> **Index), and torn into thin strips**
> **¼ cup pine nuts, toasted (see Index)**
> **2 tablespoons finely chopped**
> **fresh chives**

Put the milk and garlic in a medium saucepan and bring to a boil over low-to-moderate heat. Reduce the heat and simmer gently about 5 minutes. Drain off and discard the milk, leaving the garlic in the pan. Add the cream and bring to a boil; reduce the heat slightly and simmer briskly until the cream is reduced by about half to coating consistency, 15 to 20 minutes.

While the cream is simmering, preheat the broiler or grill until hot. About 5 minutes before the cream is reduced, brush the scallops with the melted butter and season with salt and white pepper; broil or grill them 4 to 5 inches from the heat until golden on the outside but still juicy within, 1 to 2 minutes per side.

With a slotted spoon, remove and discard the garlic from the reduced cream. Season the sauce to taste with salt and white pepper.

Spoon the sauce over cooked pasta and top with the scallops. Arrange the pepper strips around the scallops. Scatter the pine nuts on top and garnish with the chives.

Serves 4–6

Calamari alla Puttanesca Fresca

❦

The traditional, spicy, rough-and-ready, "whore-style" pasta sauce of Italy warmly welcomes tender little pieces of fresh squid in this topping that looks beautiful against the jet-black background of squid ink pasta. Ask your fishmonger to clean the squid for you, saving you the ink sacs for the pasta dough. The topping is also especially good with spinach or cornmeal pasta.

6 tablespoons extra-virgin olive oil

1¼ pounds cleaned squid, bodies cut into ¼-inch-thick rings, tentacles cut into small clusters

½ pound thinly sliced prosciutto, cut crosswise into ¼-inch-wide strips

4 medium garlic cloves, coarsely chopped

2 medium onions, coarsely chopped

2 small hot green chilies, coarsely chopped with seeds

1 teaspoon crushed red pepper flakes

1 28-ounce can whole tomatoes, including liquid

1 tablespoon double-concentrate tomato paste

1 tablespoon sugar

1 tablespoon dried oregano

1 teaspoon dried rosemary

1 bay leaf

Salt

Freshly ground black pepper

3 tablespoons finely shredded fresh basil leaves

In a large skillet, heat half the oil over moderate heat. Add the squid and sauté just until it turns white, about 1 minute. Transfer to a bowl and set aside.

Add the remaining oil to the skillet. Add the prosciutto, garlic, onions, chilies, and red pepper flakes; sauté over moderate heat until the prosciutto begins to brown, about 5 minutes.

Add the tomatoes, breaking them up with your hands. Stir in the tomato paste, sugar, oregano, rosemary, and bay leaf. Simmer briskly until thick, 15 to 20 minutes.

During the last minute or so of simmering, stir the squid pieces into the sauce. Remove the bay leaf. Season to taste with salt and pepper.

Spoon the sauce over cooked pasta and garnish with the basil.

Serves 4–6

Crab Cakes and Ginger Cream

❦

The rich ginger-infused sauce gives an intriguing Asian twist to this treatment for squid ink pasta. This also works well with red bell pepper, carrot, cornmeal, or lemon pasta.

1¼ pounds cooked flaked crabmeat
2 eggs, well beaten
½ cup mayonnaise
½ cup fine fresh bread crumbs
¼ cup finely chopped fresh chives
Salt
White pepper
2 large Roma tomatoes, cored, peeled,
   halved, seeded (see Index), and
   finely chopped
2 tablespoons finely chopped fresh
   Italian parsley
½ cup sake (Japanese rice wine)
2 medium shallots, finely chopped
2½ cups heavy cream
¼ cup finely grated fresh gingerroot
½ to 1 teaspoon fresh lemon juice
¼ cup (½ stick) unsalted butter,
   cut into pieces
¼ cup vegetable oil
¼ cup all-purpose flour
3 lemons, cut into wedges

For the crab cakes, in a mixing bowl, lightly stir together the crabmeat, eggs, mayonnaise, bread crumbs, chives, and salt and white pepper to taste. A heaping tablespoon at a time, scoop up the mixture and, with your hands, shape into round patties about ½ inch thick. Put on a waxed paper–lined tray, cover with more waxed paper, and refrigerate for at least 1 hour.

In a small bowl, toss together the tomatoes and parsley; season to taste with salt and white pepper. Cover and refrigerate.

For the sauce, in a medium saucepan, bring the sake and shallots to a boil over high heat; continue boiling until the sake has reduced to about 2 tablespoons, about 5 minutes. Add the cream, ginger, and lemon juice, bring to a boil, and reduce by about a third, 7 to 10 minutes more.

While the sake and then the cream are reducing, cook the crab cakes. Melt the butter with the oil in a large skillet over moderate heat. Lightly dust the cakes on both sides with the flour and fry them until golden brown, 3 to 5 minutes per side. Drain on paper towels and keep warm.

Pour the sauce through a fine-mesh strainer to remove the ginger. Taste the sauce and adjust its seasoning, adding a few drops of juice from one of the lemon wedges if you like.

Immediately pour the sauce over individual portions of cooked pasta and top with the crab cakes. Garnish with the tomato-parsley mixture. Pass the lemon wedges for guests to squeeze on to taste.

Serves 4–6

Herb Pasta

Herb Pasta

Goat Cheese, Sun-Dried Tomatoes, and a Hint of Anchovy

Grilled Chicken Breast in Lemon Cream

Grilled Veal Tenderloin and Sun-Dried Tomato Cream

Lamb and Porcini Bolognese

Veal Sauté with Orange Zest and Sour Cream

Fresh Mozzarella with Fresh Tomatoes

Herb Pasta

☙

Flecks of fresh herbs brightly speckle this pasta dough. Vary your choice of herbs, as suggested in the recipes in this chapter, to complement the ingredients in the sauce or topping. Basil, parsley, dill, rosemary, oregano, and tarragon are all good choices. For an even more aromatic pasta, pulse 1 or 2 garlic cloves with the herbs.

¾ cup packed fresh herbs
2 to 3 cups all-purpose flour
3 extra-large eggs
½ teaspoon salt
1 to 2 tablespoons heavy cream

Put the herbs in a food processor fitted with the metal blade and pulse until finely chopped, stopping several times to scrape down the bowl.

Add 2½ cups of the flour and the eggs and salt and process just until they form a ball of smooth dough that rides around the bowl on the blade, about 1 minute. If the dough seems too sticky, sprinkle in a little of the flour and pulse it in; if it seems too dry and does not form a ball, drizzle in a little of the cream.

Turn the dough out onto a floured work surface and continue as directed in the pasta-making instructions detailed in "Pasta and Sauce Basics."

Makes 1¼ to 1½ pounds fresh pasta; 4–6 servings

Goat Cheese, Sun-Dried Tomatoes, and a Hint of Anchovy

❧

There's a straightforward Mediterranean quality to this simple topping for basil pasta. Leave out the anchovies, if you wish. A tablespoon or two of pine nuts may be added as an extra garnish. This is also good with other herb pastas or spinach, red bell pepper, or lemon pasta.

2 tablespoons unsalted butter
2 medium shallots, finely chopped
1 cup heavy cream
1 pound fresh creamy goat cheese,
  at room temperature
4 anchovy fillets, finely chopped
½ cup sun-dried tomato pieces,
  cut into ¼-inch-wide strips
2 tablespoons finely shredded
  fresh basil

Melt the butter in a medium saucepan or skillet over moderate heat. Add the shallots and sauté until tender, 2 to 3 minutes.

Add the cream and bring to a boil. Reduce the heat to a bare simmer and drop in the goat cheese in small clumps. Add the anchovies and sun-dried tomatoes and stir until the cheese has almost but not completely melted.

Toss gently with cooked pasta and garnish with the basil.

Serves 4–6

Grilled Chicken Breast in Lemon Cream

❦

The chicken and rich lemon sauce both go very well with tarragon pasta. Try this also with oregano or basil herb pasta or with spinach pasta.

> 6 tablespoons (¾ stick) unsalted
>   butter, cut into pieces
> 2 medium shallots, finely chopped
> 6 tablespoons fresh lemon juice
> 1½ cups heavy cream
> ½ cup chicken broth
> 1½ pounds boneless, skinless
>   chicken breasts
> Salt
> White pepper
> 1 tablespoon thinly shredded fresh
>   basil leaves
> 1 tablespoon finely chopped
>   fresh chives
> 1 tablespoon finely chopped fresh
>   Italian parsley

Preheat the grill or broiler until very hot.

Meanwhile, in a medium-to-large saucepan or skillet, melt the butter over moderate heat; pour off and reserve half. Add the shallots and sauté until tender, 2 to 3 minutes.

Add the lemon juice and raise the heat slightly. When the lemon juice has almost evaporated, stir in the cream and broth; gently boil until thick but still fairly liquid, 12 to 15 minutes.

While the mixture is boiling, brush the chicken breasts with the reserved butter and season with salt and white pepper. Grill or broil the chicken until golden, about 7 minutes per side.

Season the cream sauce to taste with salt and white pepper. Toss gently with cooked pasta and place individual portions on plates or in bowls. Cut the chicken breasts crosswise into ½-inch-wide strips and arrange on top. Garnish with the basil, chives, and parsley.

Serves 4–6

Grilled Veal Tenderloin and Sun-Dried Tomato Cream

❀

The sauce, intensely colored and flavored with sun-dried tomatoes, goes especially well with fresh basil pasta. Try it, too, with spinach, cornmeal, or lemon pasta.

*¼ cup (½ stick) unsalted butter, cut
  into pieces
2 medium shallots, finely chopped
3 cups heavy cream
½ cup sun-dried tomato pieces,
  well drained
2 teaspoons dried oregano
1 bay leaf
1½ pounds veal tenderloin, trimmed
Salt
White pepper
¼ cup pine nuts, toasted (see Index)
2 tablespoons finely chopped
  fresh chives
2 tablespoons finely chopped fresh
  Italian parsley*

Preheat the grill or broiler.

Meanwhile, in a medium saucepan or skillet, melt the butter over moderate heat. Pour off and reserve half the butter.

Add the shallots to the remaining butter in the pan and sauté 1 to 2 minutes. Add the cream, sun-dried tomatoes, oregano, and bay leaf. Bring to a boil, then reduce the heat slightly and simmer briskly, stirring occasionally, until the mixture has reduced by about a third, 15 to 20 minutes.

When the cream is about half reduced, brush the veal with the reserved melted butter and season with salt and white pepper. Grill or broil until golden brown and done medium, about 5 minutes per side.

Remove the bay leaf from the cream and pour the cream and tomato mixture into a food processor fitted with the metal blade. Process until the tomatoes are pureed. Season to taste with salt and white pepper.

Gently toss the sauce with cooked pasta and place individual portions on plates or in bowls. Cut the veal diagonally into ¼-inch-thick slices and drape them on top. Sprinkle with the pine nuts and garnish with the chives and parsley.

Serves 4–6

Lamb and Porcini Bolognese

❀

The lamb in this variation on the classic Italian meat sauce makes a good match with pasta flavored with fresh rosemary or basil. The sauce is also good with bell pepper, carrot, or lemon pasta.

½ cup dry red wine
¼ cup dried porcini mushrooms
¼ cup olive oil
2 medium garlic cloves,
   finely chopped
1 large onion, finely chopped
1 pound lean ground lamb
1 28-ounce can whole tomatoes,
   including liquid
2 tablespoons double-concentrate
   tomato paste
1 tablespoon dried oregano
½ tablespoon dried basil
1 bay leaf
2 teaspoons sugar
Salt
Freshly ground black pepper
2 tablespoons finely chopped fresh
   Italian parsley

Put the red wine and mushrooms in a small bowl and leave to soak.

In a large skillet or saucepan, heat the oil over moderate heat. Add the garlic and onion and sauté until tender, 2 to 3 minutes.

Add the lamb and raise the heat slightly. Sauté until the lamb has lost all its pink color and left a brown glaze on the pan, about 10 minutes.

Meanwhile, remove the mushrooms from the wine and chop coarsely. Pour the wine through a strainer lined with a double layer of cheesecloth set over a bowl or cup.

Add the strained wine to the skillet and stir and scrape the bottom of the pan with a wooden spoon to dissolve the pan deposits. Add the tomatoes, breaking them up with your hands. Stir in the chopped mushrooms, tomato paste, oregano, basil, bay leaf, and sugar. Gently boil until thick, 15 to 20 minutes. Remove the bay leaf. Season to taste with salt and pepper.

Toss the sauce gently with cooked pasta and garnish with the parsley.

Serves 4–6

Veal Sauté with Orange Zest and Sour Cream

❦

The mild sweetness of the veal and orange zest stand up very well to parsley-garlic or basil-garlic pasta. Other good pasta choices include saffron, spinach, or carrot.

¼ cup (½ stick) unsalted butter,
  cut into pieces
2 tablespoons corn or peanut oil
2 medium shallots, finely chopped
1 pound thin veal scallops, cut into
  ½-inch-wide strips
¾ cup medium-dry white wine
¼ cup orange juice
1 bay leaf
2 cups sour cream
2 tablespoons finely grated fresh
  orange zest
Salt
White pepper
2 tablespoons finely chopped
  fresh chives

In a large skillet, melt the butter with the oil over moderate heat. Add the shallots and sauté until tender, 2 to 3 minutes.

Raise the heat to high and add the veal. Sauté until lightly browned, 3 to 5 minutes. Remove the veal from the skillet and set aside.

Add the wine, orange juice, and bay leaf to the skillet, stirring and scraping to dissolve the pan deposits. Boil until reduced by about three quarters, about 10 minutes.

Add the sour cream to the skillet along with the reserved veal. Reduce the heat and simmer, stirring frequently, until the sauce is thick and the veal has heated through, 3 to 5 minutes more. Remove the bay leaf. Stir in the orange zest and season to taste with salt and white pepper.

Gently toss the sauce with cooked pasta and garnish with the chives.

Serves 4–6

Fresh Mozzarella with Fresh Tomatoes

❀

This uncooked sauce for oregano pasta will be at its best if you use the freshly made mozzarella—preferably from buffalo milk, known as buffalo mozzarella—found floating in water in well-stocked cheese counters and Italian delis. It also works well with spinach, lemon, or other herb pasta.

1 pound firm ripe Roma tomatoes, cored, peeled, seeded (see Index), and coarsely chopped
1 teaspoon sugar
1 pound fresh mozzarella cheese, well drained and cut into ¼- to ½-inch cubes
4 medium shallots, finely chopped
6 tablespoons extra-virgin olive oil

¼ cup fresh lemon juice
2 tablespoons finely chopped fresh Italian parsley
2 tablespoons finely shredded fresh basil leaves
Salt
White pepper
Freshly grated Parmesan cheese

In a mixing bowl, toss the chopped tomato with the sugar. Add the ingredients through the basil leaves and toss well, seasoning to taste with salt and white pepper.

Leave the mixture at room temperature while you cook and drain the pasta. Add the sauce to the pasta and toss gently. Pass the Parmesan for guests to add to taste.

Serves 4–6

Lemon Pasta

Lemon Pasta

Alder-Smoked Salmon, Eggs, Gruyère Cheese, and Chives

Grilled Swordfish Fillets with Spring Vegetable Marinara

Exotic Mushroom and Asparagus Sauté

Sesame Chicken with Ginger Beurre Blanc

Lamb Sauté with Fresh Sage and Creamy Goat Cheese

Grilled Pork Tenderloin with Barbecue Marinara

Sautéed Eggplant with Sun-Dried Tomatoes, Olives, and Capers

Grilled Summer Vegetables with Oil, Garlic, and Fresh Herbs

Lemon Pasta

❦

Fresh lemon juice and grated zest add their spark to this pasta. For an interesting flavor contrast, try including 1 tablespoon of freshly ground black pepper in the mixture. You could, instead, also add some fresh basil or parsley.

> **2 to 3 cups all-purpose flour**
> **3 extra-large eggs**
> **¼ cup fresh lemon juice**
> **2 tablespoons finely grated fresh**
> **lemon zest**
> **½ teaspoon salt**
> **1 to 4 tablespoons heavy cream**

Put 2½ cups of the flour and the eggs, lemon juice, lemon zest, and salt in a food processor fitted with the metal blade. Process just until they form a ball of smooth dough that rides around the bowl on the blade, about 1 minute. If the dough seems too sticky, sprinkle in a little of the flour and pulse it in; if it seems too dry and does not form a ball, drizzle in a little of the cream.

Turn the dough out onto a floured work surface and continue as directed in the pasta-making instructions detailed in "Pasta and Sauce Basics."

Makes 1¼ to 1½ pounds fresh pasta; 4–6 servings

Alder-Smoked Salmon, Eggs, Gruyère Cheese, and Chives

❦

This brunch-style pasta scramble is especially good served with a lemon–black pepper pasta cut into angel hair. Rather than using conventional smoked salmon from the gourmet counter or deli case, I like it with the meatier chunks of canned or vacuum-packed salmon smoked in alder wood available in well-stocked markets and specialty stores; substitute flaked smoked trout, if you wish. Try the recipe as well with tomato, bell pepper, herb, cornmeal, or squid ink pasta.

8 eggs
¼ cup half-and-half or light cream
¼ pound finely shredded Gruyère
   cheese
½ teaspoon salt
¼ cup (½ stick) unsalted butter

2 6½-ounce cans alder-smoked
   salmon, drained and broken up
   into large flakes
¼ cup finely chopped fresh chives
2 tablespoons salmon roe

In a mixing bowl, lightly beat the eggs. Beat in the half-and-half, Gruyère, and salt.

In a large skillet, melt the butter over low-to-moderate heat. Add cooked and drained pasta and pour the egg mixture over it. Cook, stirring and tossing gently but continuously, until the egg begins to curdle and coat the pasta. Add the salmon and chives and continue to stir and toss gently just until the eggs are cooked but still creamy.

Transfer to individual serving plates and garnish with the salmon roe. Serve immediately.

Serves 4–6

Grilled Swordfish Fillets with Spring Vegetable Marinara

❦

Satisfyingly meaty, grilled swordfish gets hearty support from a tomato sauce packed with fresh vegetables. Instead of the lemon pasta, you can try this topping with squid ink, spinach, or herb pasta.

6 tablespoons extra-virgin olive oil

2 tablespoons fresh lemon juice

1½ pounds fresh swordfish fillet,
   cut into 1-inch-thick slices

2 medium garlic cloves,
   finely chopped

1 medium onion, finely chopped

1 28-ounce can whole tomatoes,
   including liquid

1 tablespoon double-concentrate
   tomato paste

1 tablespoon finely chopped fresh
   Italian parsley

1 tablespoon finely chopped
   fresh oregano

1 tablespoon sugar

2 bay leaves

¼ pound mushrooms, cut into
   ¼-inch-thick slices

½ cup shelled peas

1 medium carrot, cut into ¼-inch dice

1 medium golden squash or zucchini,
   cut into ¼-inch dice

Salt

White pepper

2 tablespoons finely shredded fresh
   basil leaves

2 tablespoons finely chopped
   fresh chives

In a shallow bowl, stir together 2 tablespoons of the olive oil with the lemon juice. Turn the swordfish fillets in the mixture and leave to marinate at room temperature about 30 minutes.

While the swordfish marinates, in a medium skillet or saucepan heat the remaining oil over moderate heat. Add the garlic and onion; sauté until tender, 2 to 3 minutes. Add the tomatoes, breaking them up with your hands. Stir in the tomato paste, parsley, oregano, sugar, and bay leaves. Raise the heat slightly and simmer until the sauce is thick, about 15 minutes.

About a third of the way through the sauce's simmering, stir in the vegetables.

Around the time the vegetables are added to the sauce, remove the swordfish from the marinade and season lightly with salt and white pepper. Broil close to the heat until golden brown, 4 to 5 minutes per side.

Remove the bay leaves from the sauce. Season to taste with salt and white pepper.

Gently toss the sauce with cooked pasta and place individual portions on plates or in bowls. Top with the grilled swordfish. Garnish with the basil and chives.

Serves 4–6

Exotic Mushroom and Asparagus Sauté

❦

Asparagus, though commercially grown and widely available in season, nonetheless possesses a wildness of flavor that makes it a perfect partner for exotic mushrooms—be they fresh porcini, chanterelle, portobello, cremini, or shiitake. You can also, of course, use regular domestic mushrooms if their wilder cousins are unavailable. The sauce is also good with carrot, spinach, tomato, or herb pasta.

½ cup (1 stick) unsalted butter,
    cut into pieces
¼ cup olive oil
4 medium shallots, finely chopped
¾ pound thin asparagus, trimmed, tips
    left whole, stalks cut diagonally
    into ¼-inch-wide strips
¾ pound fresh porcini, chanterelle,
    cremini, shiitake, or portobello
    mushrooms, trimmed and cut into
    ¼-inch-wide slices
6 tablespoons heavy cream
Salt
White pepper
2 tablespoons finely chopped
    fresh chives
2 tablespoons thinly shredded fresh
    basil leaves

In a large skillet or a wok, melt the butter with the oil over moderate-to-high heat. Add the shallots and sauté about 1 minute.

Add the asparagus and mushrooms and sauté, stirring briskly, until they are cooked tender-crisp, 3 to 5 minutes. Add the cream and stir about 1 minute more, until it lightly coats the vegetables.

Season to taste with salt and white pepper and gently toss the vegetables and sauce with cooked pasta. Garnish with the chives and basil.

Serves 4–6

Sesame Chicken
with Ginger Beurre Blanc

❧

Lemon pasta inspires a nouvelle variation on an Asian favorite, as strips of sesame-coated chicken are accompanied by a classic French-style sauce made exotic with grated ginger. This is also good with squid ink, red bell pepper, or carrot pasta.

2 egg whites

3 tablespoons cornstarch

1 tablespoon corn oil

1 tablespoon dry sherry

1 teaspoon salt

½ teaspoon white pepper

1¼ pounds boneless, skinless
  chicken breasts, cut crosswise
  into ¼-inch-thick slices

1 cup sesame seeds

¼ cup dry white wine

¼ cup rice vinegar

1 medium shallot, finely chopped

1 tablespoon finely grated
  fresh gingerroot

½ cup (1 stick) unsalted butter,
  cut into pieces

Salt

White pepper

Corn oil for deep frying

1 medium scallion, cut crosswise into
  thin slices

2 tablespoons coarsely chopped
  cilantro leaves

In a blender or a food processor fitted with the metal blade, process the egg whites, cornstarch, corn oil, sherry, salt, and white pepper until smoothly blended. Transfer to a bowl, add the chicken breast strips, and toss well to coat. Cover with plastic wrap and refrigerate for 1 to 2 hours.

Spread the sesame seeds on a baking sheet or platter. Turn the marinated chicken strips in the seeds to coat them evenly, pressing firmly. Transfer to a baking sheet or platter lined with waxed paper, cover with another sheet of waxed paper, and refrigerate 1 to 2 hours more to allow the sesame coating to set.

Put the wine, rice vinegar, shallot, and ginger in a medium saucepan. Bring to a boil over high heat and continue boiling until the liquid has reduced to about 2 tablespoons. Remove the pan from the heat and, with a wire whisk, briskly beat in the butter a piece at a time to form a smooth, creamy sauce. Season to taste with salt and white pepper. Keep warm.

In a deep, heavy skillet or deep fryer, heat about 3 inches of corn oil to 350°F on a deep-frying thermometer. Carefully add the chicken slices, in batches if necessary to avoid crowding, and cook until the seeds are a uniform light gold in color, 2 to 3 minutes. Remove with a skimmer or slotted spoon and drain on paper towels; skim any stray seeds from the oil and fry further batches.

Gently toss cooked pasta with the sauce and arrange individual portions on plates or in bowls. Arrange the chicken strips on top and garnish with the scallions and cilantro.

Serves 4–6

Lamb Sauté with Fresh Sage and Creamy Goat Cheese

❀

Tender scallops of lamb blend with melted creamy goat cheese and a strong suggestion of sage in this intensely flavored counterpoint to the zest of fresh lemon pasta. The topping also goes very well with spinach, tomato, bell pepper, cornmeal, or saffron pasta.

6 tablespoons (¾ stick) unsalted
   butter, cut into pieces
2 tablespoons corn or peanut oil
2 medium shallots, finely chopped
2 medium garlic cloves, finely
   chopped
2 tablespoons thinly shredded
   fresh sage leaves
1¼ pounds lamb tenderloin, cut into
   thin scallops and then cut crosswise
   into ½-inch-wide strips
½ cup dry white wine
1 bay leaf
¾ pound fresh creamy goat cheese,
   at room temperature
¼ cup heavy cream
Salt
White pepper
Whole fresh sage leaves, for garnish

In a large skillet, melt the butter with the oil over moderate heat. Add the shallots, garlic, and shredded sage leaves and sauté until tender, 2 to 3 minutes.

Raise the heat to high and add the lamb. Sauté until lightly browned, 3 to 5 minutes. Remove the lamb from the skillet and set aside.

Add the wine and bay leaf to the skillet, stirring and scraping to dissolve the pan deposits. Boil until reduced by about three quarters, about 7 minutes.

Add the goat cheese and cream to the skillet and stir until the cheese has melted and blended with the other ingredients. Add the reserved lamb, reduce the heat, and simmer, stirring frequently, until the sauce is thick and the lamb has heated through, about 3 minutes more. Remove the bay leaf. Season to taste with salt and white pepper.

Gently toss the sauce with cooked pasta and garnish with a few whole fresh sage leaves.

Serves 4–6

Grilled Pork Tenderloin with Barbecue Marinara

❧

Old-fashioned southern barbecue inspired this new-fashioned topping for lemon pasta. Try it, too, with bell pepper, spinach, or cornmeal pasta.

¼ cup vegetable oil
4 medium garlic cloves, finely
  chopped
1 medium red onion, finely chopped
1 medium green bell pepper, halved,
  stemmed, seeded, and cut into
  ¼-inch dice
1 28-ounce can crushed tomatoes
⅓ cup cider vinegar
⅓ cup packed brown sugar
1 tablespoon double-concentrate
  tomato paste
1 tablespoon dried oregano
½ tablespoon dried rosemary
2 bay leaves
1½ pounds pork tenderloin, trimmed
Salt
Freshly ground black pepper
2 tablespoons finely chopped
  fresh chives

In a medium skillet or saucepan, heat the oil over moderate heat. Add the garlic, red onion, and bell pepper; sauté until tender, 3 to 5 minutes.

Add the tomatoes, vinegar, sugar, tomato paste, oregano, rosemary, and bay leaves. Raise the heat slightly and simmer until the sauce is thick, about 15 minutes.

Meanwhile, preheat the grill or broiler until very hot.

When the sauce is almost done, lightly brush some of it all over the pork tenderloin. Keep the rest of the sauce warm.

Season the pork with salt and pepper and grill or broil until golden brown and done medium, about 5 minutes per side.

Remove the bay leaves from the sauce. Season the sauce to taste with salt and pepper and toss it gently with cooked pasta. Place individual portions on plates or in bowls. Cut the pork diagonally into ¼-inch-thick slices and drape them over each serving. Garnish with the chives.

Serves 4–6

Sautéed Eggplant with Sun-Dried Tomatoes, Olives, and Capers

❧

Reminiscent of a ratatouille, this sauce features Mediterranean flavors that are naturally complemented by lemon pasta. Try it also with spinach, green bell pepper, or herb pasta.

6 tablespoons extra-virgin olive oil
2 tablespoons unsalted butter
4 medium garlic cloves, finely
    chopped
1 pound Japanese or small globe
    eggplants, peels left on, cut into
    ½- to 1-inch chunks
3/4 cup sun-dried tomato pieces,
    drained if necessary, cut into
    ¼-inch-wide strips
3/4 cup pitted black olives
1/2 cup dry white wine
2 tablespoons capers, drained
1 tablespoon dried oregano
1 bay leaf
Salt
Freshly ground black pepper
2 tablespoons finely chopped fresh
    Italian parsley
2 tablespoons finely shredded fresh
    basil leaves

In a large skillet or saucepan, heat the oil and butter over moderate heat. Add the garlic and, as soon as it sizzles, reduce the heat to low and add the eggplant. Sauté until the eggplant begins to soften and the garlic starts to brown, 2 to 3 minutes.

Add the sun-dried tomatoes, olives, wine, capers, oregano, and bay leaf. Cover and simmer gently, stirring occasionally, until the eggplant is tender and the sauce is thick, 15 to 20 minutes. Remove the bay leaf.

With a wooden spoon, gently press on the eggplant pieces to mash them slightly. Season to taste with salt and pepper. Toss gently with cooked pasta and garnish with the parsley and basil.

Serves 4–6

Grilled Summer Vegetables with Oil, Garlic, and Fresh Herbs

❧

This presentation is particularly attractive for a summertime meal, the quickly grilled vegetables forming a colorful pattern atop fresh lemon pasta. Try the topping as well on tomato, spinach, beet, carrot, or fresh herb pasta.

1¾ cups extra-virgin olive oil
¼ cup fresh lemon juice
¼ cup finely chopped fresh Italian parsley
¼ cup finely chopped fresh chives
¼ cup finely chopped fresh basil
2 medium zucchini, trimmed and cut lengthwise into ¼-inch-thick slices
2 medium golden squash, trimmed and cut lengthwise into ¼-inch-thick slices
¼ pound fresh shiitake mushrooms or large domestic mushrooms, stems removed, caps left whole

1 dozen small scallions, root ends and top half of greens trimmed and discarded
1 large red bell pepper, halved, stemmed, and seeded, halves cut into 6 slices each
2 Japanese eggplants, trimmed and cut lengthwise into ¼-inch-thick slices
Salt
Freshly ground black pepper
4 medium garlic cloves, finely chopped
Freshly grated Parmesan cheese

In a large bowl, stir together ½ cup of the oil with the lemon juice and half each of the parsley, chives, and basil. Add the zucchini, squash, mushrooms, scallions, and bell pepper and turn them to coat. Add the eggplant and turn to coat. Leave to marinate at room temperature.

Preheat the grill or broiler until very hot.

Season the vegetables on both sides with salt and pepper and arrange on the grill or broiler tray. Cook close to the heat until golden brown, 1 to 2 minutes per side.

While the vegetables are cooking, in a large skillet heat the remaining oil with the garlic over high heat. As soon as the garlic starts to turn golden, 3 to 4 minutes, pour the oil and garlic over cooked pasta, add the remaining parsley, chives, and basil, and gently toss. Place individual portions on plates or in bowls. Arrange the grilled vegetables attractively on top and pass the Parmesan for guests to add to taste.

Serves 4–6

Saffron Pasta

Saffron Pasta

Shrimp Sauté with Spinach and Roma Tomatoes

Steamed Mussels in White Wine and Garlic Broth

Paella-Style Chicken with Tomatoes, Peppers, and Green Olives

Kashmir-Style Creamy Chicken Curry

Grilled Lamb Tenderloin with Yogurt Raita

Saffron Pasta

❦

Threads of saffron contribute an intense golden color and unmistakable perfume to this fresh pasta. The saffron can be costly, but it's worth the investment for a special meal.

> **3 extra-large eggs**
> **2 teaspoons saffron threads**
> **2 to 3 cups all-purpose flour**
> **½ teaspoon salt**
> **2 to 4 tablespoons heavy cream**

In a mixing bowl, lightly whisk together the eggs and saffron. Set aside for about 5 minutes.

Put 2½ cups of the flour and the eggs and salt in a food processor fitted with the metal blade. Process just until they form a ball of smooth dough that rides around the bowl on the blade, about 1 minute. If the dough seems too sticky, sprinkle in a little of the flour and pulse it in; if it seems too dry and does not form a ball, drizzle in a little of the cream.

Turn the dough out onto a floured work surface and continue as directed in the pasta-making instructions detailed in "Pasta and Sauce Basics."

Makes 1¼ to 1½ pounds fresh pasta; 4–6 servings

Shrimp Sauté with Spinach and Roma Tomatoes

❧

An elaboration on the concept of scampi-style shrimp, this colorful medley couldn't be quicker to prepare, and the heady perfume of saffron pasta adds just the grace note. The sauté also goes well with fresh herb, lemon, or squid ink pasta.

1 cup extra-virgin olive oil
½ cup (1 stick) unsalted butter,
   cut into pieces
6 medium garlic cloves,
   finely chopped
¾ pound medium shrimp,
   shelled and deveined
2 cups packed spinach leaves,
   stemmed, thoroughly washed,
   and cut crosswise into ½-inch-
   wide strips

4 large Roma tomatoes, cored,
   peeled, halved, seeded (see Index),
   and coarsely chopped
2 tablespoons fresh lemon juice
Salt
Freshly ground black pepper
Freshly grated Parmesan cheese

In a large skillet, heat the olive oil and butter over moderate-to-high heat. Add the garlic and sauté about 30 seconds.

Add the shrimp and sauté about 2 minutes. Add the spinach and tomatoes; sauté until the shrimp are uniformly pink and the spinach has just wilted, about 2 minutes more. Sprinkle in the lemon juice and season to taste with salt and pepper.

Toss gently with cooked pasta and place individual portions on plates or in bowls. Pass the Parmesan for guests to add to taste.

Serves 4–6

Saffron Pasta

Steamed Mussels in
White Wine and Garlic Broth

❦

Aromatic, golden saffron pasta provides a lovely background for this classic French treatment of fresh shellfish. You could, if you like, substitute fresh clams for the mussels. This also goes well with squid ink, spinach, or tomato pasta.

6 tablespoons unsalted butter,
   cut into pieces
¼ cup extra-virgin olive oil
8 medium garlic cloves,
   finely chopped
3 cups dry white wine
2 bay leaves
1 teaspoon dried oregano
1 teaspoon dried rosemary
3 dozen fresh mussels, well scrubbed
   and soaked in cold water
Salt
White pepper
¼ cup finely chopped fresh
   Italian parsley
2 tablespoons finely chopped
   fresh chives
2 tablespoons finely chopped
   fresh basil

In a large pot over moderate heat, melt the butter with the oil. Add the garlic and sauté 1 minute. Add the wine and bay leaves; crumble in the oregano and rosemary. Bring to a boil and reduce the heat to a brisk simmer.

Add the mussels, cover the pot, and cook until all the shells have opened, 5 to 7 minutes. Remove the mussels with a slotted spoon to a covered bowl. Discard any unopened mussels.

Pour the liquid from the pot through a strainer lined with a double layer of cheesecloth and set over a large bowl. Rinse out the pot and return the strained liquid to it. Bring it back to a simmer over moderate heat. Season to taste with salt and white pepper.

Arrange the mussels on top of individual portions of cooked pasta and sprinkle with the parsley, chives, and basil. Ladle the hot liquid over the mussels and pasta.

Serves 4–6

Paella-Style Chicken with Tomatoes, Peppers, and Green Olives

❧

The Spanish specialty known as paella features rice colored and scented with saffron. So it's not too long a leap to create a quick chicken breast pasta sauce seasoned in the style of paella to be served over saffron pasta. This sauce is also good with spinach, bell pepper, lemon, or fresh herb pasta.

6 tablespoons extra-virgin olive oil

6 medium garlic cloves, finely chopped

1 small green bell pepper, stemmed, seeded, and cut into ½-inch squares

1 small red bell pepper, stemmed, seeded, and cut into ½-inch squares

1 small onion, coarsely chopped

1 pound boneless, skinless chicken breasts, cut crosswise into ½-inch-wide strips

1 tablespoon Spanish paprika

½ cup dry sherry

1 28-ounce can whole tomatoes, including liquid

¾ cup pimiento-stuffed green olives, each cut crosswise in half

¼ cup coarsely chopped fresh Italian parsley

1 tablespoon double-concentrate tomato paste

2 teaspoons sugar

2 teaspoons dried oregano

2 bay leaves

In a large skillet or saucepan, heat half the oil over high heat. Add the garlic, bell peppers, and onion; sauté until tender and just beginning to brown, 3 to 5 minutes. Remove the vegetables and set them aside.

Add the remaining oil to the skillet and heat over high heat; add the chicken and sauté until it just begins to turn golden, 2 to 3 minutes. Just before the chicken is done, sprinkle evenly with the paprika and sauté about 1 minute more.

Add the sherry and stir and scrape to deglaze the skillet. Add the tomatoes, breaking them up with your hands. Stir in the olives, half the parsley, the tomato paste, sugar, oregano, and bay leaves. Simmer until the sauce is thick but still slightly liquid, about 20 minutes. Remove the bay leaves.

Spoon the sauce over cooked pasta and toss gently. Garnish with the remaining parsley.

Serves 4–6

Kashmir-Style
Creamy Chicken Curry

❦

Saffron pasta beautifully takes over the role of the rice pilaf that would ordinarily be served with such a curry. The mild and subtly spiced sauce may come as a revelation to those who have previously shied away from Indian food.

¼ cup (½ stick) unsalted butter,
    cut into pieces
2 tablespoons vegetable oil
1½ pounds boneless, skinless chicken
    breasts, cut into ½-inch chunks
1 medium onion, coarsely chopped
1 small red bell pepper, stemmed,
    seeded, and cut into ½-inch dice
1 small green bell pepper, stemmed,
    seeded, and cut into ½-inch dice
3 tablespoons mild curry powder
2 teaspoons grated fresh gingerroot
1½ cups heavy cream

¼ cup seedless golden raisins
¼ cup dried apricots, cut into
    ¼-inch dice
Salt
White pepper
¼ cup toasted shredded coconut
½ cup whole or halved cashew nuts,
    toasted (see Index)
¼ cup slivered almonds, toasted
    (see Index)
2 tablespoons coarsely chopped
    cilantro leaves

In a large skillet over moderate heat, melt half the butter with half the oil. When the butter foams, add the chicken pieces and sauté until lightly browned, 3 to 5 minutes. Remove from the skillet and set aside.

Add the remaining butter and oil to the skillet and sauté the onion and bell peppers for 1 to 2 minutes; sprinkle in the curry powder and ginger and sauté about 1 minute more. Add the cream and stir and scrape to dissolve the pan deposits. Return the chicken to the skillet, stir in the raisins and apricots, and simmer gently until thick, 5 to 7 minutes more. Season to taste with salt and white pepper.

Gently toss some of the cream sauce with cooked pasta and pour the rest of the sauce and chicken on top. Sprinkle with the toasted coconut, then scatter with the cashews, almonds, and cilantro.

Serves 4–6

Grilled Lamb Tenderloin with Yogurt Raita

❀

Use low-fat, nonfat, or whole-milk yogurt, depending on your preference, for the cool sauce that backs up this Indian-style grilled lamb. In place of saffron pasta, you could serve this on carrot, lemon, or spinach pasta.

2 cups plain yogurt
2 tablespoons medium-hot curry
   powder
1 tablespoon fresh lemon juice
1 tablespoon grated fresh gingerroot
1½ pounds lamb tenderloin, well
   trimmed
Salt
White pepper
2 pickling cucumbers, peels left on,
   coarsely shredded
1 small red onion, finely chopped
1 tablespoon finely chopped fresh
   chives
1 tablespoon finely chopped cilantro
   leaves
1 tablespoon finely chopped fresh
   mint leaves
1 tablespoon lime juice
¼ cup pine nuts or cashew nut halves,
   toasted (see Index)

Saffron Pasta

In a mixing bowl, stir together ¾ cup of the yogurt with the curry powder, lemon juice, and ginger. Add the lamb and turn to coat it well. Marinate at room temperature for 30 minutes.

While the lamb marinates, preheat the grill or broiler until very hot.

Season the lamb with salt and white pepper and grill or broil close to the heat until well charred but still slightly rare inside, 4 to 5 minutes per side.

While the lamb is cooking, make the raita by stirring together the remaining yogurt with the cucumber, red onion, herbs, and lime juice. Season to taste with salt and white pepper.

Gently toss cooked pasta with the raita and place individual portions on plates or in bowls. Cut the lamb crosswise into ¼-inch-thick slices and arrange them on top. Garnish with the pine nuts or cashews.

Serves 4–6

Chocolate Pasta

Chocolate Pasta

Ground Turkey Mole

Fresh Raspberry Coulis

Vanilla Ice Cream and Hot Chocolate Truffle Sauce

Kirsch-Soaked Sun-Dried Cherries and Confectioners' Sugar

Marmalade Butter and Grand Marnier

Almond Crème Brûlée

Lime Caramel

Chocolate Pasta

❧

*This recipe yields a pasta with the color of rich fudge. Omit the sugar if you wish to
serve the pasta with a savory topping.*

> **2 to 3 cups all-purpose flour**
> **½ cup unsweetened cocoa powder**
> **½ cup confectioners' sugar**
> **½ teaspoon salt**
> **3 extra-large eggs**
> **2 to 4 tablespoons heavy cream**

Put 2 cups of the flour with the cocoa powder, sugar, and salt in a food
processor fitted with the metal blade and pulse the machine until they are
thoroughly blended. Add the eggs and process until they form a ball of
smooth dough that rides around the bowl on the blade, about 1 minute. If
the dough is too soft, pulse in a little more of the flour; if it is too stiff and
does not form a ball, drizzle in some of the cream.

Turn the dough out onto a floured work surface and continue
as directed in the pasta-making instructions detailed in "Pasta and
Sauce Basics."

Makes 1¼ to 1½ pounds fresh pasta; 4–6 servings

Ground Turkey Mole

❦

This version of a classic Mexican sauce gains a richness from the traditional inclusion of unsweetened chocolate—which makes it ideal for serving with chocolate pasta that omits the sugar. Try it, too, with cornmeal, red bell peppers, tomato, or spinach pasta.

¼ cup olive oil
4 medium garlic cloves,
   finely chopped
1 medium red onion, finely chopped
1 pound ground turkey
1 28-ounce can whole tomatoes,
   including liquid
1 ounce unsweetened baking
   chocolate, coarsely chopped
1 medium red bell pepper, stemmed,
   seeded, and cut into ½-inch squares

1 medium green bell pepper, stemmed,
   seeded, and cut into ½-inch squares
1 tablespoon double-concentrate
   tomato paste
1 tablespoon dried oregano
½ tablespoon sugar
½ teaspoon salt
3 tablespoons finely chopped cilantro

In a large skillet or saucepan, heat the oil over moderate heat. Add the garlic and red onion and sauté until tender, 2 to 3 minutes.

Add the ground turkey. Raise the heat slightly. Sauté until the meat has lost its pink color and has left a brown glaze on the pan, about 10 minutes. Add the tomatoes, breaking them up with your hands. Stir and scrape the bottom of the pan with a wooden spoon to dissolve the pan deposits.

Stir in the chocolate, bell peppers, tomato paste, oregano, sugar, and salt. Gently boil until thick, 15 to 20 minutes. Serve over cooked pasta and garnish with the cilantro.

Serves 4–6

Fresh Raspberry Coulis

❀

Make this when fresh raspberries are at the peak of the season. The same sauce made with strawberries or blackberries will complement sweet chocolate pasta equally well.

2½ cups fresh raspberries
¼ cup (½ stick) unsalted butter,
  cut into pieces
¼ to ½ cup confectioners' sugar
1 tablespoon fresh lemon juice
Fresh mint sprigs, for garnish

Put 2 cups of the raspberries in a food processor fitted with the metal blade. Pulse several times, then process until the berries are uniformly pureed. Pour the puree through a fine-mesh sieve, pressing it with a wooden spoon to extract all the puree; discard the seeds left behind in the sieve.

In a medium saucepan, melt the butter over low-to-moderate heat; sprinkle in ¼ cup of the confectioners' sugar, stirring to dissolve it completely. Add the raspberry puree and cook, stirring frequently, just until the sauce is heated through. Stir in the lemon juice. Taste and, if necessary, sprinkle and stir in more of the sugar.

Toss gently with cooked pasta and garnish with the remaining whole raspberries and the mint sprigs.

Serves 6

Vanilla Ice Cream and
Hot Chocolate Truffle Sauce

❃

Especially decadent, this treatment for sweet chocolate pasta employs the best store-bought vanilla ice cream you can find, coupled with a quickly prepared, creamy fudge sauce.

½ **pound imported semisweet chocolate, broken into pieces**

¾ **cup heavy cream**

¼ **cup framboise (raspberry liqueur) or other fruit liqueur**

¼ **cup (½ stick) unsalted butter, cut into pieces**

4 **tablespoons confectioners' sugar**

1½ **pints good-quality vanilla ice cream**

Fresh mint sprigs, for garnish

In the top of a double boiler over a gentle simmer, melt the chocolate, stirring occasionally with a wire whisk.

While the chocolate melts, in a small saucepan over moderate heat, bring the cream to a boil. Remove the top half of the double boiler and, whisking the chocolate continuously, slowly pour in the cream. Stir in the framboise.

Rinse and dry the small saucepan and use it to melt the butter. Gently toss the butter with cooked chocolate pasta, sprinkling in the confectioners' sugar; serve individual portions in bowls. Top each serving with a scoop of ice cream and drizzle with the chocolate sauce. Garnish with the mint sprigs.

Serves 6

Kirsch-Soaked Sun-Dried Cherries and Confectioners' Sugar

❦

Resembling raisins in shape, tart-sweet sun-dried or kiln-dried cherries are becoming more readily available in specialty food stores and are well worth seeking out for this vivid-tasting topping for sweet chocolate pasta.

> 1 cup kirsch (cherry brandy)
> 1¼ cups sun-dried pitted cherries
> 1 cup (2 sticks) unsalted butter,
>   cut into pieces
> 6 tablespoons slivered almonds,
>   toasted (see Index)
> ½ cup confectioners' sugar

Put the kirsch in a small saucepan and warm over low heat until barely hot. Add the cherries and leave to soak for 30 minutes, stirring occasionally. Drain well.

In a small skillet, melt the butter over low heat. Add the soaked, drained cherries and sauté just until heated, 1 to 2 minutes.

Spoon the cherries and butter over cooked chocolate pasta and toss gently. Garnish individual portions with the almonds. Put the confectioners' sugar in a fine-mesh sieve and shake over each portion to dust generously.

Serves 6

Marmalade Butter and Grand Marnier

❀

Marmalade, sweet and fragrant but with a hint of bitterness from the Seville oranges from which it is made, goes wonderfully with the flavor of sweet chocolate pasta. A splash of Grand Marnier or some other orange-flavored liqueur gives the sauce extra aromatic punch; most of the alcohol evaporates in the heat of the pan. You can also garnish with a few fresh seasonal berries, if you like.

1 cup (2 sticks) unsalted butter, cut into pieces
1 cup good-quality thin-shred orange marmalade, at room temperature
6 tablespoons Grand Marnier or other orange liqueur
Fresh mint sprigs, for garnish

In a medium saucepan or skillet, melt the butter over low heat. Add the marmalade and Grand Marnier and stir until the mixture has just heated through.

Toss gently with cooked pasta and garnish with the mint sprigs.

Serves 6

Almond Crème Brûlée

❀

The secret behind this presentation is to arrange an even bed of cooked sweet chocolate pasta in each of 6 shallow, broilerproof serving bowls and then completely cover them with the custard mixture. When guests break through the burnt-sugar crust formed on top of each, the hidden chocolate pasta comes as a delightful surprise.

> **2½ cups heavy cream**
> **6 large egg yolks**
> **¼ cup granulated sugar**
> **1 teaspoon cornstarch**
> **1 teaspoon pure almond extract**
> **½ teaspoon pure vanilla extract**
> **1 cup light-brown sugar**

In a medium saucepan over low-to-moderate heat, heat the cream just until bubbles begin to form along its edge. Remove from the heat.

In a mixing bowl, beat the egg yolks with a wire whisk until they are smooth and lemon yellow. In a separate bowl, stir together the granulated sugar and cornstarch; beating the yolks continuously, gradually sprinkle in the sugar mixture. Still whisking, slowly pour in the hot cream.

In the top of a double boiler over gently simmering water, cook the mixture, stirring frequently, until it forms a custard thick enough to coat a wooden spoon, 15 to 20 minutes. Remove from the heat and stir in the almond and vanilla extracts. Let cool to room temperature, stirring occasionally.

Arrange cooked chocolate pasta evenly in the bottoms of 6 individual broilerproof serving dishes. Pour the cooled custard on top, smoothing its surface. Cover with plastic wrap and refrigerate.

About 15 minutes before serving, heat the broiler. Evenly sprinkle the brown sugar over the surface of each serving. Place the serving dishes on a baking sheet and slide under the broiler; watch carefully. When the sugar topping has completely melted and started to bubble, 2 to 3 minutes, remove immediately. Let cool a few minutes before serving.

Serves 6

Lime Caramel

❦

Luscious, *a word overused in cookbooks, probably best describes this rich, creamy, ever-so-slightly tangy sauce for sweet chocolate pasta. The clever idea of adding a touch of lime to caramel was taught to me by one of my best friends, the brilliant chef John Sedlar.*

> *2 cups heavy cream*
> *1 cup granulated sugar*
> *1 tablespoon water*
> *¼ cup fresh lime juice*
> *1 teaspoon pure vanilla extract*

In a mixing bowl, whisk 1 cup of the cream until it forms soft peaks. Cover and refrigerate. Leave the remaining 1 cup of cream at room temperature.

In a heavy, medium skillet put the sugar and water over moderate heat. Stir until the sugar melts; then leave it to cook undisturbed until the sugar has turned a medium caramel brown, 10 to 15 minutes. Watch carefully to be sure that the caramel doesn't burn.

The moment the caramel reaches the desired color, very carefully stir in the room-temperature cream with a wooden spoon. When it is fully incorporated, remove the pan from the heat. Stir in the lime juice and vanilla.

Pour the sauce over cooked pasta. Garnish with the whipped cream.

Serves 6

Index

Index

166

Peppercorn Cream, Bell
Pepper Pasta and, 21
Wild, Parmesan Cream Sauce,
Tomato Pasta and, 94
Mussels Steamed in White Wine
Garlic Broth, Saffron Pasta
and, 146

New Mexican Green Chili with
Pork, Cornmeal Pasta and,
54
nuts, toasted, 5

olive oil, 6
Oysters, Creamed, with Jalapeño
Salsa Fresca, Squid Ink Pasta
and, 104

Paella-Style Chicken with
Tomatoes, Peppers, and
Green Olives, Saffron Pasta
and, 148
Pancetta, Crispy, and Pine Nuts,
White Wine Cream with,
Spinach Pasta and, 69
Parmesan
Brown Butter, and Parsley,
Carrot Pasta and, 44
Cream, Caviar, Basil, and
Pine Nuts, with Lobster
Tails, Bell Pepper Pasta
and, 26
Cream Sauce, Wild
Mushroom, Tomato Pasta
and, 94
Crème Fraîche, and Chives,
Beet Pasta and, 18
Shavings and Tuna, with
Rustic Anchovy-Olive
Tapenade, Bell Pepper
Pasta and, 24
Sirloin Meatballs with Black
Pepper Butter and,
Tomato Pasta and, 84
Pasta, basics
about cutting, drying,
kneading, rolling,
shaping, storing, 1–3
baby food for, 1
cooking and serving, 3–4, 7

flavorings and seasonings for,
4–7
tomatoes for, 7
Pasta, Fresh. *See also* Name of
Fresh Pasta
Beet, 10
Bell Pepper, 20
Carrot, 38
Chocolate, 156
Cornmeal, 46
Herb, 114
Lemon, 126
Saffron, 145
Spinach, 60
Squid Ink, 98
Tomato, 74
Peas, Baby, and Smoked Gouda
Cream, Beet Pasta and, 17
Peas, Peppers, and Goat Cheese
Cream Sauce, Grilled
Chicken with, Tomato Pasta
and, 78
Pepper(s). *See also* BELL PEPPER
PASTA; Chili Peppers
about roasting, 6
Bell, and Pine Nuts, Shrimp
Scampi with, Spinach
Pasta and, 61
Bell, Roasted, and Exotic
Mushroom Medley,
Tomato Pasta and, 88
Peas, and Goat Cheese Cream
Sauce, Grilled Chicken
with, Tomato Pasta and,
78
Roasted, and Garlic Cream,
Seared Sea Scallops with,
Squid Ink Pasta and, 106
Roasted, and Spicy Shrimp,
Tomato Pasta and, 75
and Sweet Italian Sausage
Sauté, Tomato Pasta and,
90
Tomatoes, and Green Olives,
Paella-Style Chicken
with, Saffron Pasta and,
148
Pesto
Avocado-Cilantro, with
Grilled Shrimp, Cornmeal
Pasta and, 50

Chili, with Grilled Red Chili-
Dusted Salmon, Cornmeal
Pasta and, 48
Rustic, with Balsamic
Vinegar, Tomato Pasta
and, 92
Spinach, with Lemon-Dill
Grilled Chicken, Beet
Pasta and, 12
Porcini Mushrooms. *See*
Mushrooms
Pork
New Mexican Green Chili
with, Cornmeal Pasta
and, 54
Red Wine, and Mushroom
Ragout, Carrot Pasta and,
39
Tenderloin, Grilled, with
Apples and Cream,
Cornmeal Pasta and, 56
Tenderloin, Grilled with
Barbecue Marinara,
Lemon Pasta and, 136
Printanier with Roma Tomatoes,
Carrot Pasta and, 42
Prosciutto with Alfredo, Bell
Pepper Pasta and, 35

Queso, Fresh Green and Red
Chilies con, Cornmeal Pasta
and, 55

Ragout, Duck and White Wine,
Tomato Pasta and, 82
Ragout, Pork, Red Wine, and
Mushroom, Carrot Pasta
and, 39
Raita, Yogurt, Grilled Lamb
Tenderloin with, Saffron
Pasta and, 152
Raspberry Coulis, Fresh,
Chocolate Pasta and, 158
Ricotta, Melted, Fresh Herbs,
Butter, and Garlic, Bell
Pepper Pasta and, 34
Ricotta, Tomato, and Basil,
Spinach Pasta and, 67
Romano Cream, Chili-Dusted,
with Bacon and Pine Nuts,
Cornmeal Pasta and, 58

Index
168

toasting nuts, 5
TOMATO PASTA, 74; DISHES
FEATURING, 75–94
Bell Pepper, Roasted, and
Exotic Mushroom Medley, 88
Chicken and Asparagus Sauté
with Lemon Butter and
Fresh Herbs, 80
Chicken, Grilled, with Goat
Cheese Cream Sauce,
Peas, and Peppers, 79
Duck and White Wine
Ragout, 82
Feta Cream with Black Olives
and Pine Nuts, 93
Rustic Pesto with Balsamic
Vinegar, 92
Sausage, Sweet Italian, and
Pepper Sauté, 90
Shrimp, Grilled Lemon-
Rosemary, with
Cannellini Beans and
Shallots, 76
Shrimp, Spicy, and Roasted
Peppers, 75
Sirloin Meatballs with Black
Pepper Butter and
Parmesan, 84
Sugar Snap Pea Sauté with
Lemon Zest, 91
Veal and Eggplant Oreganato,
86
Wild Mushroom Parmesan
Cream Sauce, 94

Tomato(es). *See also* Sun-Dried
Tomatoes
about canned, concentrate,
and fresh, 7
Fresh, Fresh Mozzarella with,
Herb Pasta and, 124
Peppers, and Green Olives,
Paella-Style Chicken
with, Saffron Pasta and,
148
Ricotta, and Basil, Spinach
Pasta and, 67
Roma, with Printanier, Carrot
Pasta and, 42
Roma and Spinach, Shrimp
Sauté with, Saffron Pasta
and, 145
Sauté, Spicy, with Melted
Goat Cheese, Spinach
Pasta and, 66
Tuna and Parmesan Shavings,
and Rustic Anchovy-Olive
Tapenade, Bell Pepper Pasta
and, 24
Tuna, Seared, and Hot Asian
Vinaigrette with Pickled
Ginger, Bell Pepper Pasta
and, 22
Turkey Mole, Ground, Chocolate
Pasta and, 157

Vanilla Ice Cream and Hot
Chocolate Truffle Sauce,
Chocolate Pasta and, 159

Veal
and Eggplant Oreganato,
Tomato Pasta and, 86
Grilled, with Dijon mustard
Cream, Bell Pepper Pasta
and, 32
Sauté with Orange Zest and
Sour Cream, Herb Pasta
and, 122
Tenderloin, Grilled, and Sun-
Dried Tomato Cream,
Herb Pasta and, 118
Vegetable(s)
Baby, Sauté, with Grilled
Beef, Bell Pepper Pasta
and, 30
Grilled Summer, with Oil,
Garlic, and Fresh Herbs,
Lemon Pasta and, 140
Marinara, Spring, Grilled
Swordfish Fillets with,
Lemon Pasta and, 128
Printanier with Roma
Tomatoes, Carrot Pasta
and, 42

White Wine Cream with Crispy
Pancetta and Pine Nuts,
Spinach Pasta and, 69
Wild Mushroom. *See* Mushrooms

Yogurt Raita, Grilled Lamb
Tenderloin with, Saffron
Pasta and, 152